marvelous

NORMAN SCHMIDT

mini kites

Sterling Publishing Co., Inc. New York
A Sterling/Tamos Book

A Sterling / Tamos Book
© 1998 Norman Schmidt

Sterling Publishing Company, Inc.
387 Park Avenue South, New York, NY 10016

TAMOS Books Inc.
300 Wales Avenue, Winnipeg, MB, Canada R2M 2S9

10   9   8   7   6   5   4   3   2   1

Distributed in Canada by Sterling Publishing Co., Inc.
c/o Canadian Manda Group, 1 Atlantic Avenue, Suite 105
Toronto, Ontario, Canada M6K 3E7
Distributed in Great Britain and Europe by Cassell PLC
Wellington House, 125 Strand, London WC2R 0BB, England
Distributed in Australia by Capricorn Link (Australia) Pty Ltd.
P.O. Box 6651, Baulkham Hills,
Business Centre, NSW 2153, Australia

Design   Norman Schmidt
Photography   Jerry Grajewski, Custom Images

Printed in China

CANADIAN CATALOGING IN PUBLICATION DATA

Schmidt, Norman, 1947-

Marvelous mini kites

"A Sterling/TAMOS book."
Includes index.
ISBN 1-895569-29-X

1. Kites – Design and construction.   I. Title.

TL759.S355 1998   629.133'32   C98-920065-5

LIBRARY OF CONGRESS
CATALOGING IN PUBLICATION DATA AVAILABLE

√ **MAI** 428-1640

2

ISBN 1-895569-29-X hardcover
     1-895569-41-9 paper

CONTENTS

3

Kites have been made in the Orient for thousands of years. When travelers first saw them many centuries ago, they carried them from one place to another, and by the 14th century kites were common throughout Europe. While on the one hand kites were important scientific devices which in the West eventually led to the invention of the airplane, in the Orient they were essentially works of folk art, important to the pastimes and festivals of all classes of people.

The first kites were improvised from bamboo and wood for military use. Later, after silk-making was discovered, this finely woven fabric was used as a sail over a bamboo frame. Silk was lightweight and could be brightly painted, making it ideal for kites. But it was an expensive material only the wealthy could afford, and for a while kite flying remained a pastime of the aristocracy. With the invention of paper, however, a more affordable material could be substituted for silk. Kite flying rapidly became a widespread public pastime.

As objects of eye-catching beauty and a means of communicating with supernatural powers, kites were flown in many ancient Chinese festivals. The Lantern Festival, celebrated on the fifteenth day of the first month of the new year, is one example. Every householder had to send the Deity of Wealth (who was thought to have descended from the heavens on New Year's Eve) back to heaven again. This was done by flying kites. At midday everyone left off other activities and the sky filled with bright and superbly painted swallows, peacocks, geese, and insects of all kinds. When darkness fell lanterns were tied to the kites, filling the heavens with twinkling lights. Strings of firecrackers were also set off, adding to the gaiety of the occasion. By midnight it was assumed the kites had completed their task. The kites were tethered and left to fly all night. By morning many had disappeared on the wind, and the people believed that these kites had carried misfortune away with them.

Because kites were so much a part of everyday life in the Orient, the art of kite making developed into a highly refined craft. To meet the ongoing demand for many kites, entire families of kite builders emerged, handing techniques down from generation to generation. The shapes of kites and the images drawn on their sails developed out of local culture, with motifs taken from folk tales and historical and religious legends. Some bore symbolic meanings such as happiness or good fortune; others were interpretations from nature. Although these paintings were usually elaborate, they were never mere decorations. All the designs had meaning and bore some special message.

I have been inspired by these kites and the brightly colored miniatures in this book are built from these and other historical examples. They are made entirely of paper, having no separate frame. Structural strength is achieved by folding, cutting, and gluing. Building these kites will acquaint the novice kite maker with some principles of kite building and aerodynamics. The materials are inexpensive and the variety of patterns allows you to make different models and experiment with decoration and design.

Aerodynamics

In simple terms, a kite rises because the moving air (wind) blowing against the face of the kite, set at a slant (angle of attack), pushes upward with a force greater than the downward gravitational pull. The kite's flying line keeps the kite from being blown backward. Instead, the air is forced to flow around the kite, its shape dividing the flow into several streams — some air is deflected downward and some to each side. The slant of the kite prevents air from flowing upward over the top. In the process of dividing and deflecting the flow of air, the airspeed decreases but its pressure is increased. Behind the kite the streams meet in turbulent flow with decreased pressure. The difference in air pressure between the front and back of the kite is what keeps the kite rising.

Thus there are four forces that counterbalance each other when a kite is airborne: the lift counterbalances the pull of gravity, while the pushing pressure of the wind against the resistance of the kite counterbalances the pull of the flying line. The force of gravity is constant (the weight of the kite); the other forces are variable. Wind varies — the lift and push vary accordingly. And the pull is controlled by the person flying the kite.

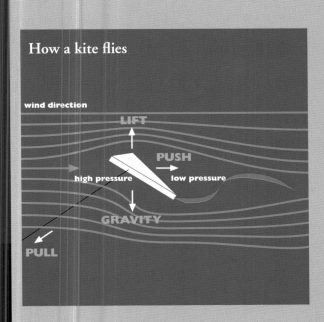

How a kite flies

wind direction

LIFT

PUSH

high pressure   low pressure

GRAVITY

PULL

Small paper kites are fragile and cannot tolerate strong or gusty wind. Neither can they tolerate rough handling. Because of their miniature size the lift they generate is small. Therefore they are not high fliers. Because paper distorts easily, they are sensitive to wind pressure and require a light touch on the kite's flying line, applying gentle give-and-take as the wind acts on the lightweight kite and line. Because they are made entirely of paper, they don't tolerate damp weather.

Launching and flying

The secret to successful kite flying lies in being able to work with the variables. The first variable is the wind. Near the ground it is always turbulent and slower than at a higher altitude (wind gradient). The second variable is the kite itself — some are more tolerant of different wind conditions; some simply fly better than others. Therefore the best way to learn kite flying is to begin with an all around easy flier, such as the first kite in this book. It is among the best fliers. It is also easy to make.

Small kites can be easily launched by one person. Stand with your back to the wind, with the line and reel in one hand, and the kite in the other. Hold the kite by its spine, with its nose pointing skyward, and let the tail (if it has one) flow freely. Raise the kite to arm's length and release it, unwinding some line as you do so, but not so much that the line goes slack. Let out more line as the kite rises. Because wind is always a bit turbulent near the ground, compensate with give-and-take on the tension of the line as you let it out, to keep pressure constant on the kite. Do not run with the kite.

If a kite has difficulty climbing, give a series of gentle but firm tugs on the line. With each tug the kite will climb a bit higher. This process can be continued until the kite reaches a height where there is stronger steadier wind.

Although the kites in this book are small, they will not fly successfully in a small space. Choose a wide open area away from buildings and trees. Obstructions of any kind make wind turbulent (wind shadow). Never fly kites near power lines or roadways.

Most kites have the following parts

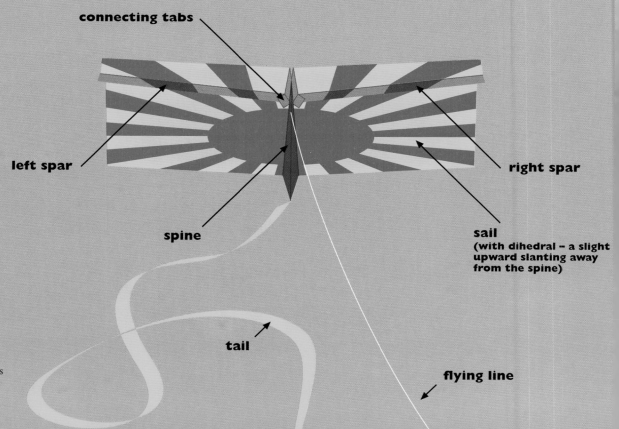

connecting tabs

left spar

right spar

spine

sail
(with dihedral – a slight upward slanting away from the spine)

tail

flying line

NOTE
The best way to store these kites is to suspend them hanging upside down from their towing point.

About paper

The kites in this book are made entirely of ordinary copy paper, which is available in standard sizes — 8½ x 11 in (21.6 x 28 cm) and 8½ x 14 in (21.6 x 35.5 cm), and standard weights — 20 or 24 lb (75 or 90 g/m²). It comes in a variety of colors. For construction follow the detailed steps given for each kite. A valley fold is one in which the crease is V-shaped. A mountain fold is the opposite, Λ-shaped. To ensure accurate folds, paper should be scored along the fold lines. This is an indentation in the paper made with a blunt tool such as a dry ball-point pen or a dull table knife.

Decorating

Adding color to a kite is an important part of kite making. Since the very beginning of kites they have been brightly decorated with a variety of motifs. It is a joy to see a beautiful shape and a splash of color waving gently in the sky. Miniature kites are no exception. Paper kites are best decorated using felt pens, since liquid paints wrinkle the paper too much. You can copy the patterns shown, using the grid method, or invent your own.

A work area should be well lit and large enough to spread things out.

Basic equipment and materials:

**cutting mat
paper
white craft glue
stapler
plastic bag
button thread
craft knife
pencil
ruler
scoring tool
compass
felt pens**

A kite's stability

Several things contribute to a kite's stability:

● **Axial symmetry** — A kite must be *exactly* the same on the left side of the spine as it is on the right side, without any twisting or warpage in the paper.

● **Dihedral** — For roll stability, a kite's sail must slant upward away from the spine. This is achieved by inserting a V-shaped spar connector at the junction of the spars and spine, between the connecting tabs. Use the following pattern to make the connector:

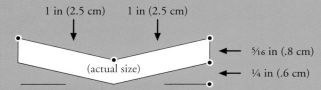

spar connector

glue up several layers of paper, or cut from lightweight card for added strength

1 in (2.5 cm)   1 in (2.5 cm)

⁵⁄₁₆ in (.8 cm)

(actual size)

¼ in (.6 cm)

the V-shape gives the kite its dihedral

● **A tail** — A kite that is wider than it is long (high aspect ratio) tends to roll and yaw more than a narrow kite. A tail provides stability. A suitable tail can be cut from a lightweight plastic shopping bag in a long spiral. A crêpe-paper streamer could also be used. Make it no wider than 1 in (2.5 cm). Depending on the wind, length should be between 3 and 10 ft (1-3 m). Attach the tail to the back of the spine using a short piece of thin wire so that it swivels freely, reinforcing the attaching point with tape.

● **Towing point** — A kite's flying line must be attached at the correct point on the spine to give the kite the best angle to the wind (pitch). This point is indicated in the instuctions for each kite. It may, however, need to be relocated up or down along the spine, depending on construction and wind. Use a large needle or a small nail to make a hole for the towing hook at the end of the line. This point may be reinforced with tape.

● **Wind** — Small paper kites cannot tolerate strong wind. If the wind is too strong or gusty they distort and spin badly. Fly them when a gentle steady breeze is blowing. The stronger the wind the longer the tail and the higher the towing point.

Handling a kite

A handy reel for holding the flying line and controlling the
kite in flight can be made from corrugated cardboard,
as shown:

towing hook
made from light
wire

flying line is
button thread (extra strong)
50 ft (15 m)

notch for line

glue
double layers

hand hold

notch for line

Size: 5 in x 5 in
(12.5 x 12.5 cm)

**Copy this pattern (shown actual size) and cut it out of
corrugated cardboard. Use a double layer, crossing the
grain direction of the two layers for strength.**

DELTA ONE

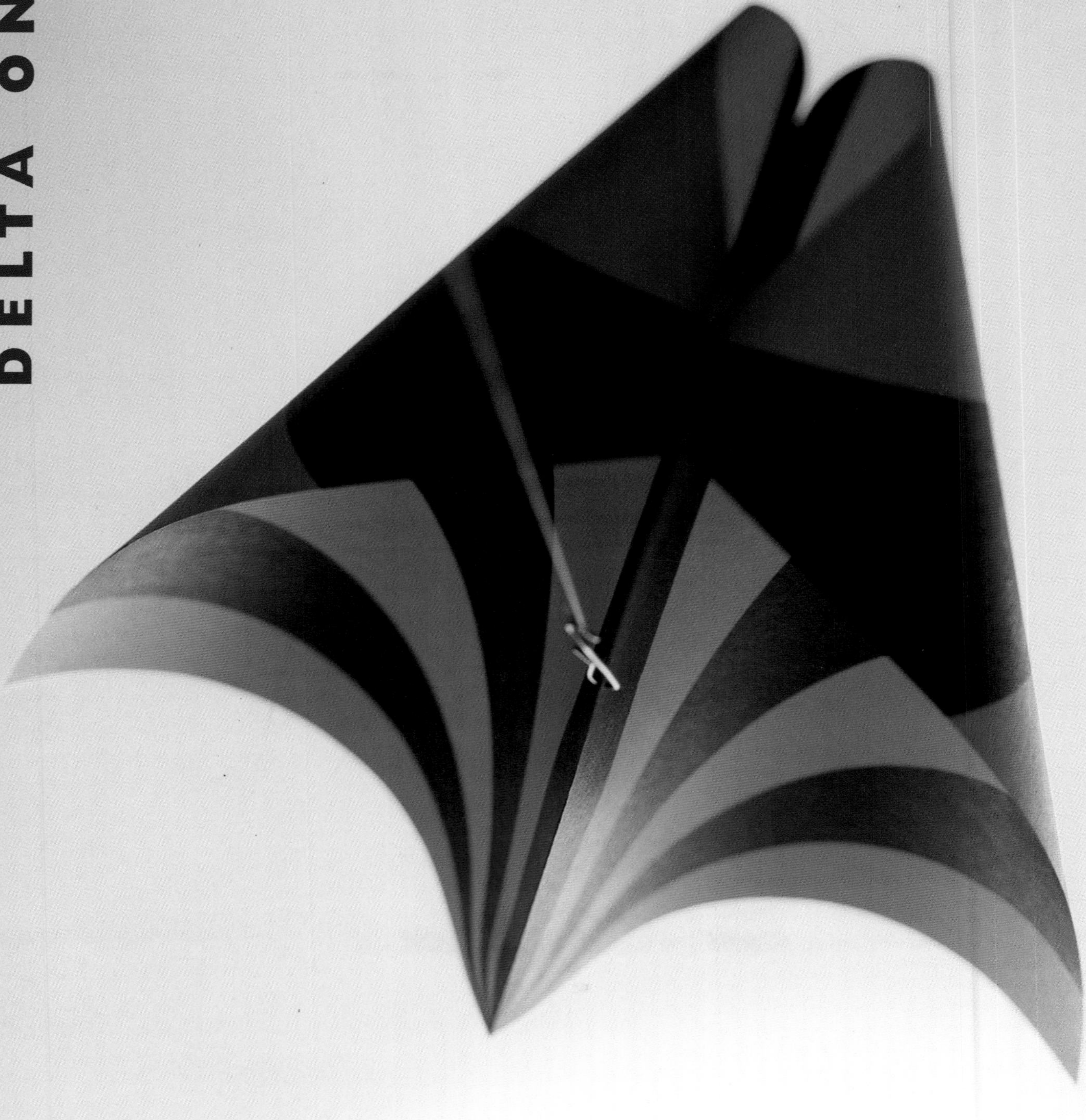

DELTA WING

The word delta comes from the Greek, meaning triangular. Objects grouped in threes have long stood for stability. Ancient Egyptian pyramids have endured because of the strength of their triangular shape. An ancient Hebrew proverb says, "a threefold cord is not quickly broken." A milking stool has three legs. Many bridges and the roof frames of houses are built with triangular beam arrangements.

The triangular shaped kite is very stable in flight. It was discovered by Francis Rogallo as a result of research done on methods of retrieving space vehicles returning to earth. The space shuttle is a delta wing aircraft.

**Paper size:
8 ¹/₂ x 11 in
(21.6 x 28 cm),
folded as shown.
Decorate before
constructing the
kite.**

**Using the grid
method, copy all
or part of this
pattern to add
color to the
kite. Or create
your own
scheme.**

draw a 1 in
(2.5 cm) grid

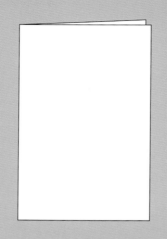

1 ¼ in
(3.1 cm)

1 Paper size: 8 ½ x 11 in (21.6 x 28 cm).
Lay paper flat in a horizontal direction.
Valley fold in half vertically. Along the fold,
measure and mark, as shown.

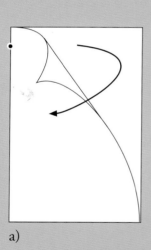

a)

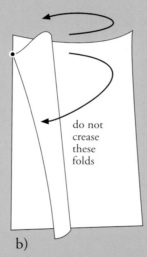

do not
crease
these
folds

b)

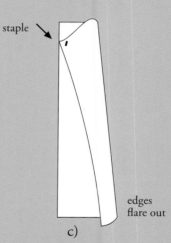

staple

edges
flare out

c)

2 On both sides, (a) fold upper right corner to the mark. (b) Do not crease the
folds. Let the free edges flare out to make the kite's sail. (c) Staple in place, as shown.
(This kite has no spars.)

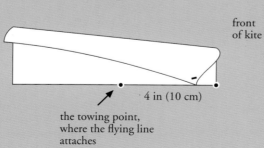

front
of kite

4 in (10 cm)

the towing point,
where the flying line
attaches

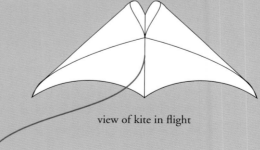

view of kite in flight

3 Measure and mark the towing point, as shown. Attach a flying line (see p 8).
This kite flies best without a tail, however, a short tail could be added for decoration.

SUN

SUN

(rectangle)

Without the sun's warmth there would be no life as we know it on earth. The sun has come to stand for origins. It is also a universal symbol of radiance and beauty. In many cultures the sun is an important artistic motif and is found in the hieroglyphics of ancient Egypt. They called the sun Ra — first ruler. To ancient Persians the sun was Mithras – truth. The sun also graces the flag of Japan. The Japanese refer to their country as Nippon — the land where the sun rises.

14

**Paper size:
8 ¹/₂ x 11 in
(21.6 x 28 cm),
folded as shown.
Decorate before
constructing the
kite.**

**Using the grid
method, copy all
or part of this
pattern to add
color to the
kite. Or create
your own
scheme.**

draw a 1 in
(2.5 cm) grid

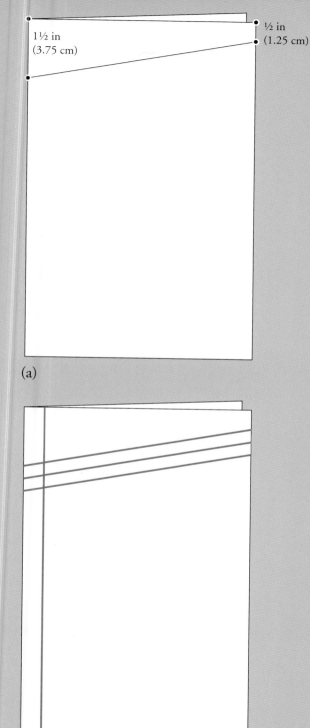

1½ in
(3.75 cm)

½ in
(1.25 cm)

(a)

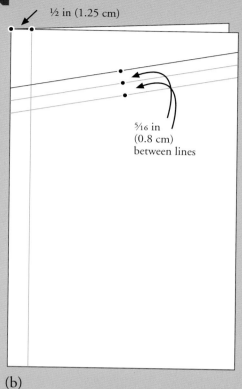

½ in (1.25 cm)

5/16 in
(0.8 cm)
between lines

(b)

1 Paper size: 8 ½ x 11 in (21.6 x 28 cm). (a) Lay paper flat in a horizontal direction. Valley fold in half vertically. Measure and draw the basic line. (b) Measure and draw fold lines, shown in orange.

2 Score the fold lines, shown in red. Make sure that both the top and bottom sheets of paper are sufficiently scored.

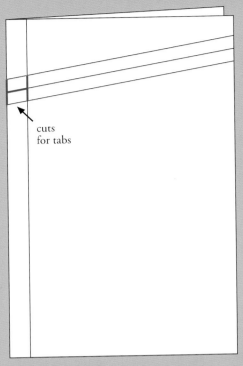

3 Cut along lines, shown in blue. Use a craft knife. Where possible, cut upper and lower sheets together, ensuring symmetry. Unfold.

cuts
for tabs

4 Valley fold along scored lines, shown in broken red. This forms the spine.

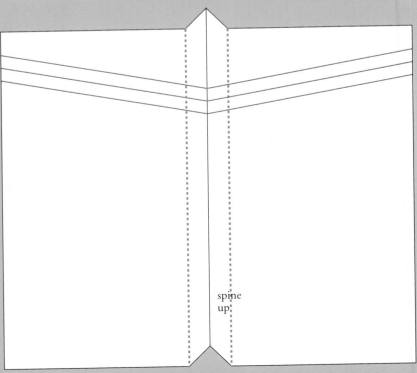

spine
up

NOTE
The unfolded kite is lying on its back with the spine up.

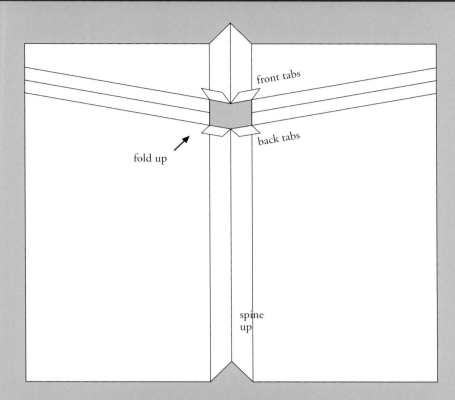

front tabs

back tabs

fold up

spine
up

5 Fold up the 4 small tabs in the spine.

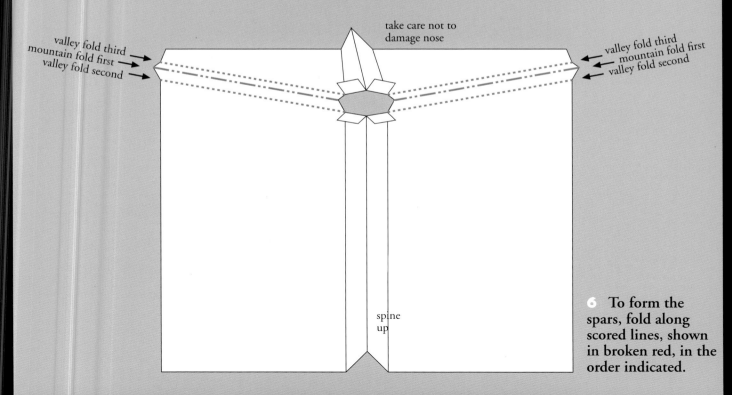

valley fold third
mountain fold first
valley fold second

take care not to
damage nose

valley fold third
mountain fold first
valley fold second

spine
up

6 To form the spars, fold along scored lines, shown in broken red, in the order indicated.

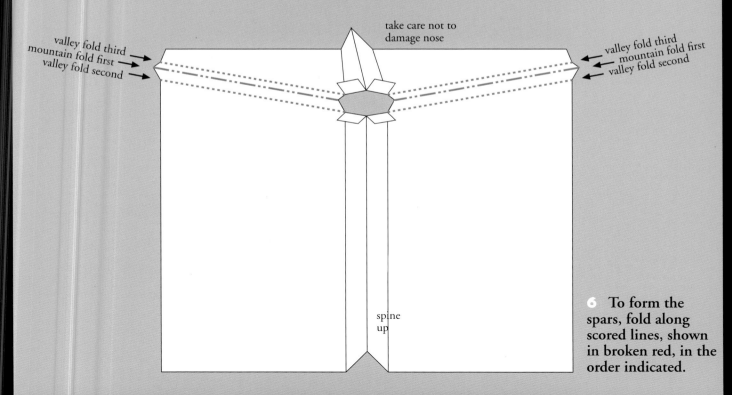

7 Glue spars and spine inside their V-shapes, as indicated.

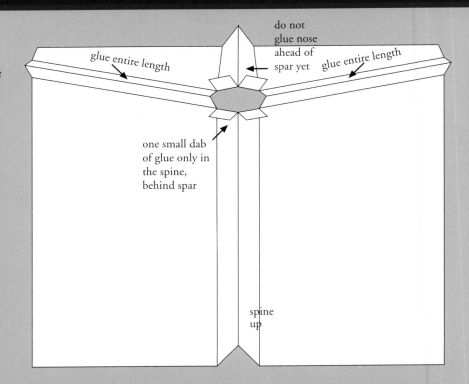

do not glue nose ahead of spar yet

glue entire length

glue entire length

one small dab of glue only in the spine, behind spar

spine up

8 Make dihedral spar connector. (See p 8.)

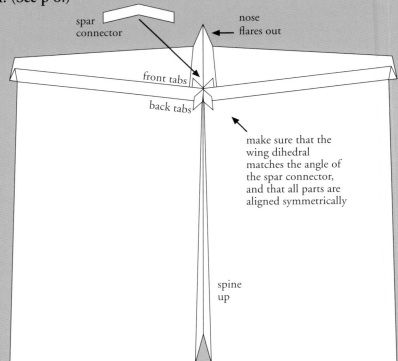

spar connector

nose flares out

front tabs

back tabs

make sure that the wing dihedral matches the angle of the spar connector, and that all parts are aligned symmetrically

spine up

9 Apply glue to the 4 tabs and the spar connector. Slide connector into place centered between the front and back tabs. Align carefully.

10 Press the junction of spars and spine firmly together and hold (or clamp) until glue has set. When all other glue is completely dry, glue the tip of the nose.

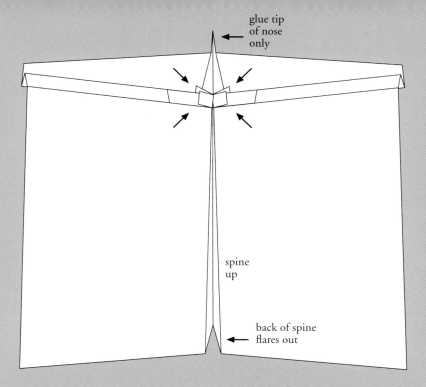

glue tip
of nose
only

spine
up

back of spine
flares out

11 For best results, the kite should be adjusted as indicated. Make sure all glue is completely dry before flying kite.

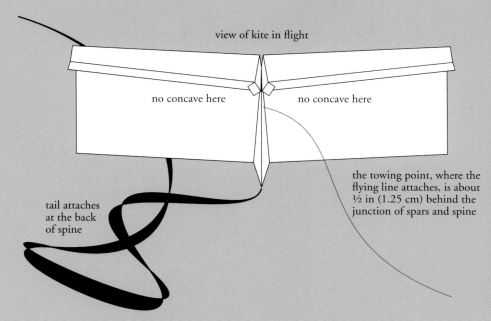

view of kite in flight

no concave here

no concave here

tail attaches
at the back
of spine

the towing point, where the flying line attaches, is about ½ in (1.25 cm) behind the junction of spars and spine

DELTA TWO

DELTA WING

An airfoil shape having a curved upper and lower surface, something like the wing of an airplane, can be incorporated into a delta kite, giving an added lift advantage to the already stable triangular kite.

draw a 1 in (2.5 cm) grid

Paper size: 8 ½ x 11 in (21.6 x 28 cm), folded as shown. Decorate before constructing the kite.

Using the grid method, copy all or part of this pattern to add color to the kite. Or create your own scheme.

1   Paper size: 8 ½ x 11 in (21.6 x 28 cm). Lay paper flat in a horizontal direction. Valley fold in half vertically. Measure and draw the spine line.

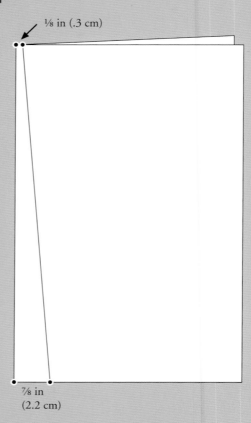

⅛ in (.3 cm)

⅞ in (2.2 cm)

2   Draw the line, shown in green. This is a guideline for step 9. Draw this line on the reverse side of the paper (inside).

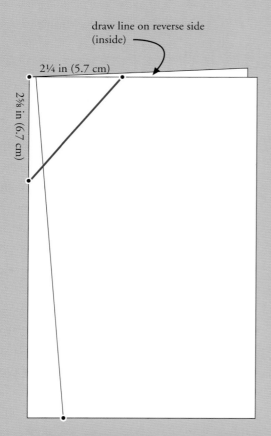

draw line on reverse side (inside)

2¼ in (5.7 cm)

2⅝ in (6.7 cm)

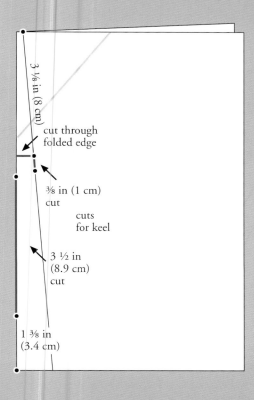

3 ⅛ in (8 cm)

cut through
folded edge

⅜ in (1 cm)
cut

cuts
for keel

3 ½ in
(8.9 cm)
cut

1 ⅜ in
(3.4 cm)

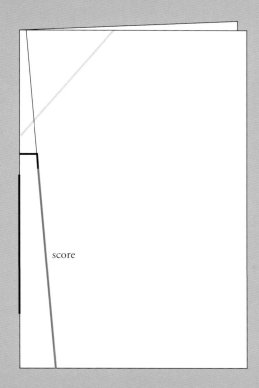

score

3 Measure and cut along lines, shown in blue. Where applicable, cut through upper and lower sheet together, ensuring symmetry. Unfold.

4 Score the bottom portion of spine fold line only, shown in red. Make sure that both the top and bottom sheets of paper are sufficiently scored.

5 Valley fold along broken lines shown in red. This forms the spine. Then reverse the fold line shown in blue (broken line), making that portion of the center crease a valley fold (see next step).

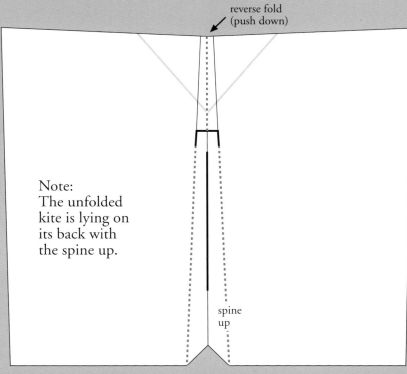

reverse fold
(push down)

Note:
The unfolded
kite is lying on
its back with
the spine up.

spine
up

view of kite in flight

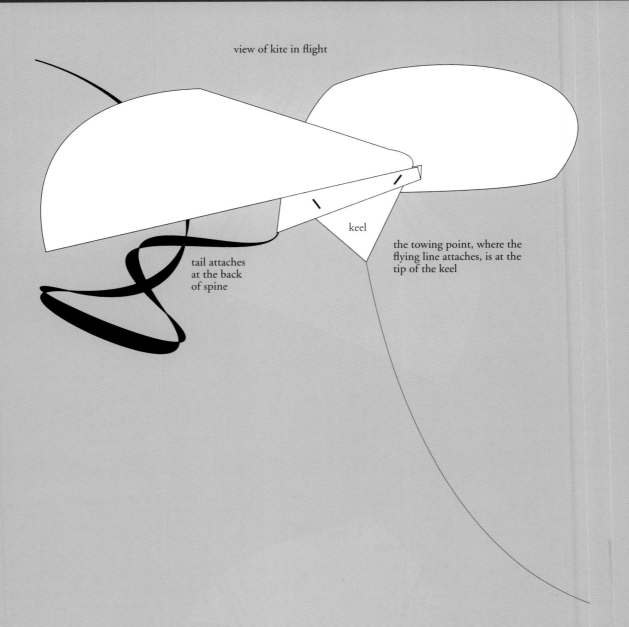

tail attaches
at the back
of spine

keel

the towing point, where the
flying line attaches, is at the
tip of the keel

10 Turn the kite over and attach the
flying line and tail for flight, as shown.

STAR

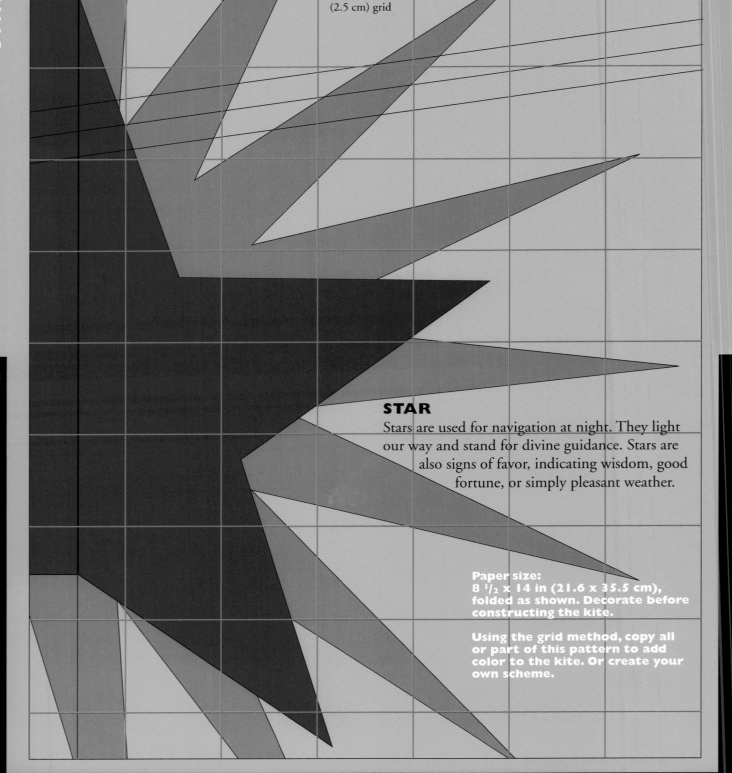

draw a 1 in
(2.5 cm) grid

STAR

Stars are used for navigation at night. They light our way and stand for divine guidance. Stars are also signs of favor, indicating wisdom, good fortune, or simply pleasant weather.

Paper size:
8 ½ x 14 in (21.6 x 35.5 cm),
folded as shown. Decorate before
constructing the kite.

Using the grid method, copy all
or part of this pattern to add
color to the kite. Or create your
own scheme.

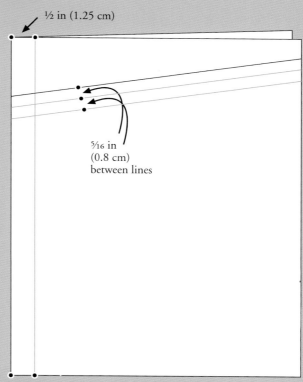

½ in (1.25 cm)

1 ½ in (1.25 cm)

½ in (1.25 cm)

(a)

⁵⁄₁₆ in (0.8 cm) between lines

(b)

1 Paper size: 8 ½ x 14 in (21.6 x 35.5 cm). (a) Lay paper flat in a horizontal direction. Valley fold in half vertically. Measure and draw the basic line. (b) Measure and draw fold lines, shown in orange.

2 Score the fold lines, shown in red. Make sure that both the top and bottom sheets of paper are sufficiently scored.

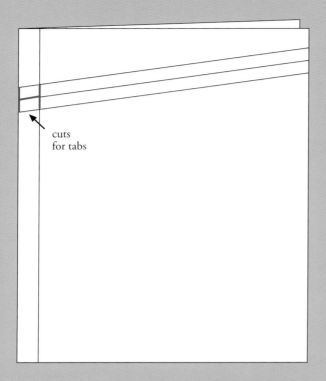

cuts
for tabs

3 Cut along lines, shown in blue. Use a craft knife. Where possible, cut upper and lower sheets together, ensuring symmetry. Unfold.

NOTE
to finish the kite
see steps 4-11 on pp 16-19.

Kite unfolded.

LEAF

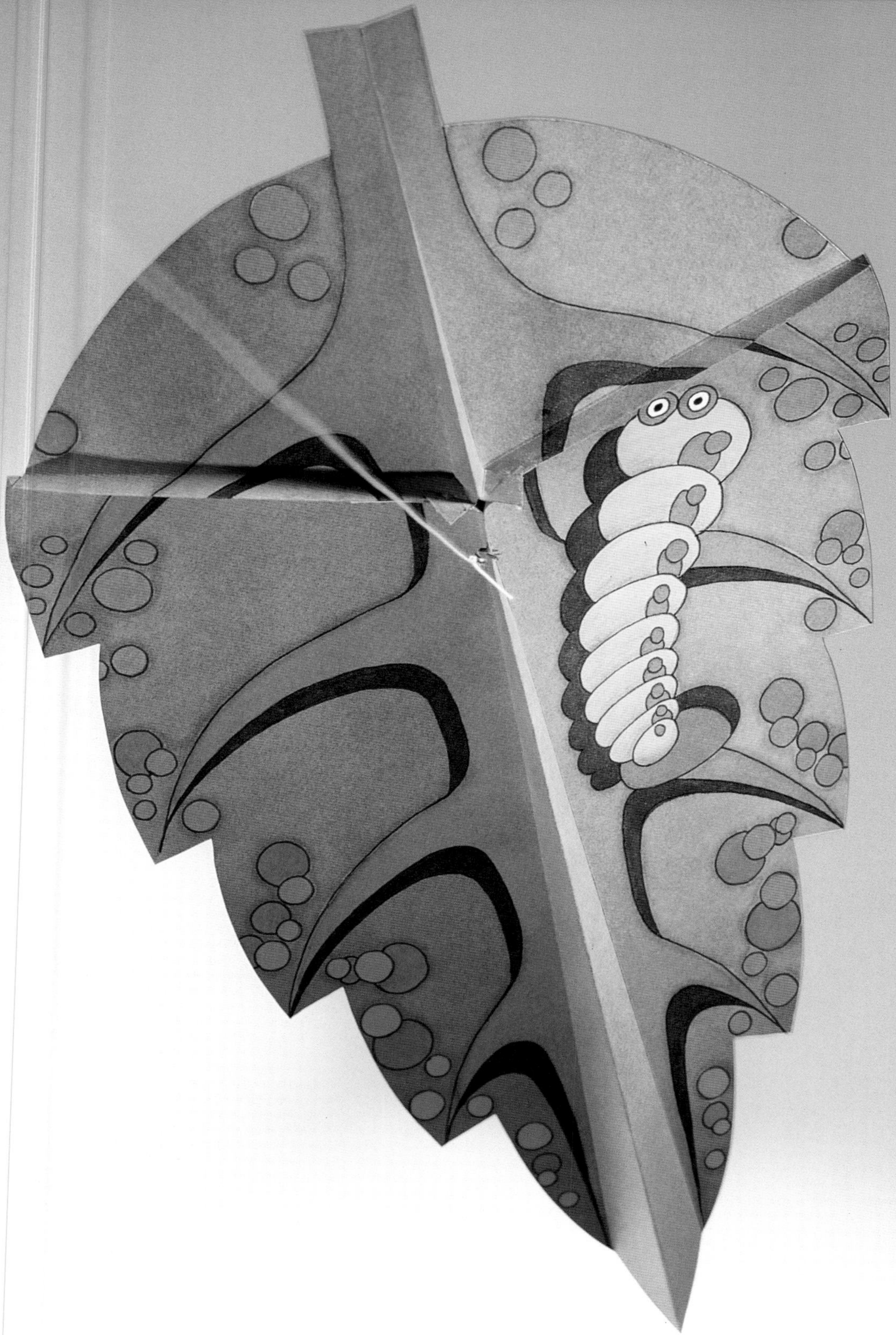

draw a 1 in
(2.5 cm) grid

LEAF
(with worm)

The green leaf means life. It is the means whereby a plant absorbs the energy from the sun. In the South Sea Islands the leaves of tropical plants are large and were probably used to make the first kites in that part of the world. These kites were used for fishing. A line with a hook at the end was tied to the kite, which was then flown out over the water with the baited hook dangling in the water to attract the fish.

**Paper size:
8 ¹/₂ x 14 in
(21.6 x 35.5 cm),
folded as shown.
Decorate before
cutting out the
kite shape.**

**Using the grid
method, copy all
or part of this
pattern to add
color to the kite.
Or create your
own scheme.**

LEAF

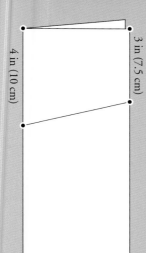

3 in (7.5 cm)

4 in (10 cm)

1 Paper size: 8 ½ x 14 in (21.6 x 35.5 cm). Lay paper flat in a vertical direction. Valley fold in half vertically. Measure and draw the basic line.

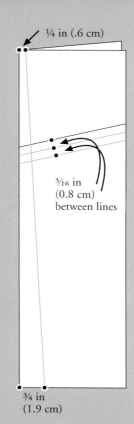

¼ in (.6 cm)

5⁄16 in (0.8 cm) between lines

¾ in (1.9 cm)

2 Measure and draw the fold lines, shown in orange.

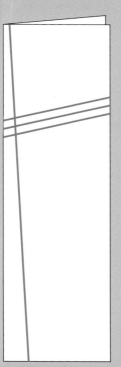

3 Score the fold lines, shown in red. Make sure that both the top and bottom sheets of paper are sufficiently scored.

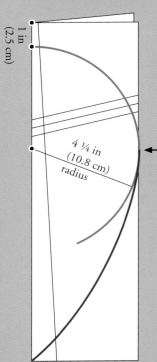

1 in
(2.5 cm)

4 ¼ in
(10.8 cm)
radius

use this
point as
reference

4 First add curved line,
shown in red. Then add
another curved line
(shown in green) drawn
freehand, using the
reference point.

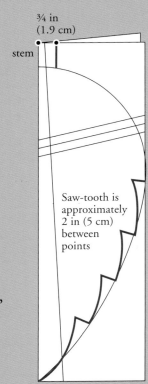

¾ in
(1.9 cm)

stem

Saw-tooth is
approximately
2 in (5 cm)
between
points

5 Measure and add the
stem line (shown in
green). The leaf saw-
tooth edge (also shown in
green) is drawn freehand,
as indicated.

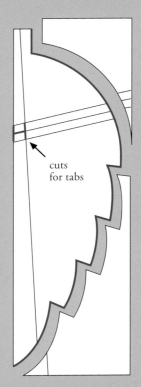

cuts
for tabs

6 Cut along lines,
shown in blue. Use a
craft knife. Where
possible, cut upper
and lower sheets
together, ensuring
symmetry. Unfold.

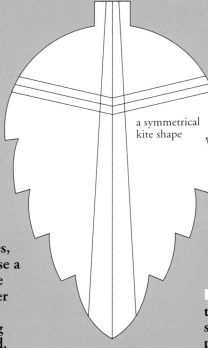

a symmetrical
kite shape

NOTE
to finish the kite
see steps 4-11 on
pp 16-19.

draw a 1 in
(2.5 cm) grid

FISH

The fish kite or windsock is seen especially in Japan, where the carp is a symbol of strength, fortitude, and success. It is flown to celebrate the birth of a child as a wish of success in life. In China the fish (especially the catfish) stands for abundance and auspiciousness. In the Christian religion the fish is a symbol of life – the letters spelling the word fish in Greek, the language of early Christians, correspond to the name of Christ.

**Paper size:
8 ¹/₂ x 14 in
(21.6 x 35.5 cm),
folded as shown.
Decorate before
cutting out the
kite shape.**

**Using the grid
method, copy all
or part of this
pattern to add
color to the kite.
Or create your
own scheme.**

FISH

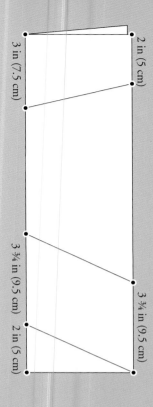

3 in (7.5 cm)

2 in (5 cm)

3 ¾ in (9.5 cm)

3 ¾ in (9.5 cm)

2 in (5 cm)

1 Paper size: 8 ½ x 14 in (21.6 x 35.5 cm). Lay paper flat in a vertical direction. Valley fold in half vertically. Measure and draw the basic lines.

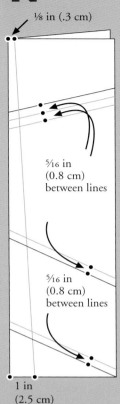

⅛ in (.3 cm)

⁵⁄₁₆ in (0.8 cm) between lines

⁵⁄₁₆ in (0.8 cm) between lines

1 in (2.5 cm)

2 Measure and draw the fold lines, shown in orange.

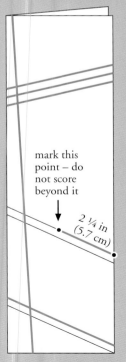

mark this point – do not score beyond it

2 ¼ in (5.7 cm)

3 Score the fold lines, shown in red. Make sure that both the top and bottom sheets of paper are sufficiently scored.

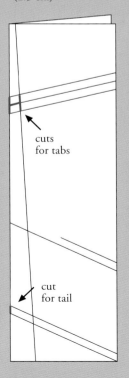

cuts for tabs

cut for tail

4 Cut along lines, shown in blue. Use a craft knife. Where possible, cut upper and lower sheets together, ensuring symmetry.

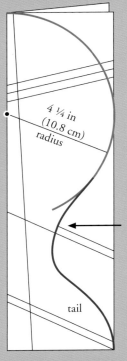

4 ¼ in
(10.8 cm)
radius

use this
point as
reference

tail

5 First add curved line, shown in red. Then add line (shown in green) drawn freehand, using the reference point.

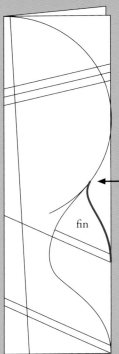

use this
point as
reference

fin

6 Add line (shown in green) drawn freehand, using the previously drawn line as reference. For steps 5 and 6, use the layout on p 36 for further reference.

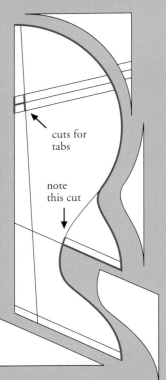

cuts for
tabs

note
this cut

7 Cut along lines, shown in blue. Use a craft knife. Where possible, cut upper and lower sheets together, ensuring symmetry. Unfold.

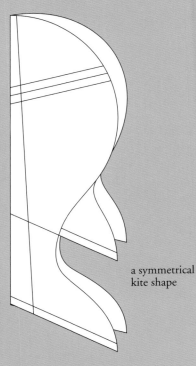

a symmetrical
kite shape

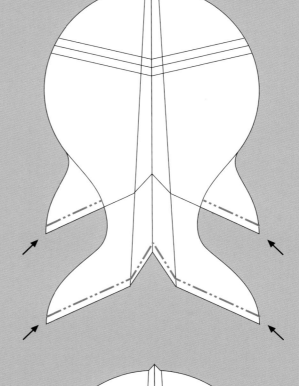

Note: The unfolded kite is lying on its back with the spine up.

spine up

8 Valley fold along broken lines, shown in red. This forms the spine.

9 Mountain fold along broken lines, shown in red, to make fin and tail stiffeners.

10 Glue the stiffeners inside their V-shape, as shown.

NOTE
to finish the kite
see steps 5-11 on pp 17-19.

glue entire length

glue entire length

glue entire length

glue entire length

spine up

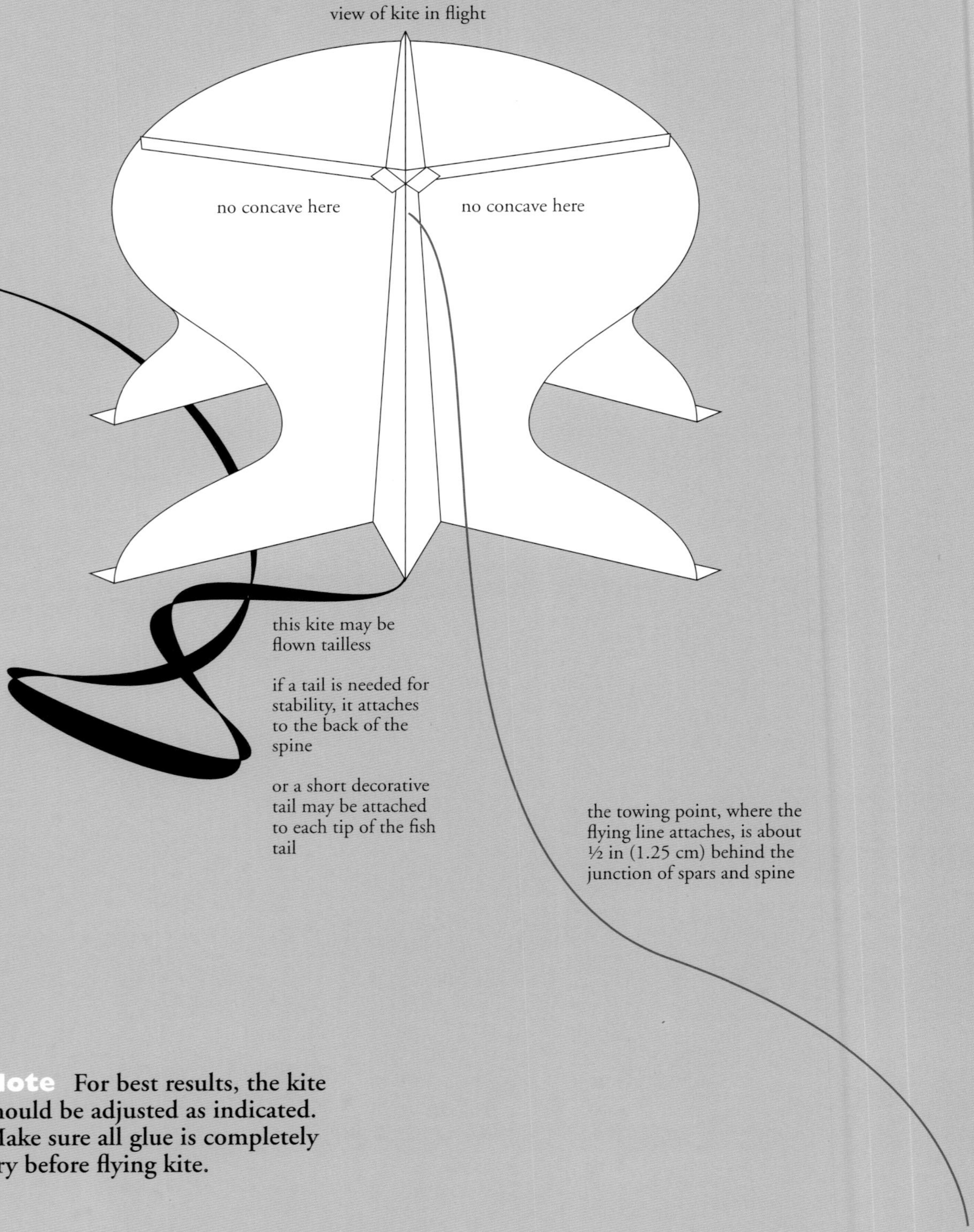

view of kite in flight

no concave here   no concave here

this kite may be
flown tailless

if a tail is needed for
stability, it attaches
to the back of the
spine

or a short decorative
tail may be attached
to each tip of the fish
tail

the towing point, where the
flying line attaches, is about
½ in (1.25 cm) behind the
junction of spars and spine

Note For best results, the kite
should be adjusted as indicated.
Make sure all glue is completely
dry before flying kite.

draw a 1 in
(2.5 cm) grid

FROG

Although the frog is a beneficial creature because its diet of insects helps control pests, in the West it has had a bad reputation because it inhabits dark cold slimy swamps, and its knobby warty skin is thought by some people to be repulsive. Therefore it has generally been a symbol of evil. In China, on the other hand, it has always been a sign of protection because it guards crops against insect infestation.

**Paper size:
8 ¹/₂ x 14 in
(21.6 x 35.5 cm),
folded as shown.
Decorate before
cutting out the
kite shape.**

**Using the grid
method, copy all
or part of this
pattern to add
color to the kite.
Or create your
own scheme.**

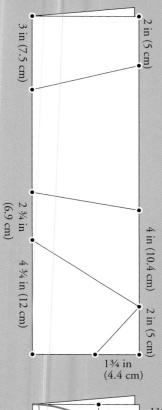

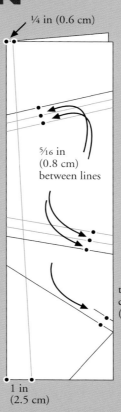

1 Paper size: 8 ½ x 14 in (21.6 x 35.5 cm). Lay paper flat in a vertical direction. Valley fold in half vertically. Measure and draw the basic lines.

3 in (7.5 cm)

2 in (5 cm)

2 ¾ in (6.9 cm)

4 in (10.4 cm)

4 ¾ in (12 cm)

2 in (5 cm)

1 ¾ in (4.4 cm)

¼ in (0.6 cm)

5/16 in (0.8 cm) between lines

this is a cut line (step 6)

1 in (2.5 cm)

2 Measure and add further lines, as indicated. Fold lines are shown in orange.

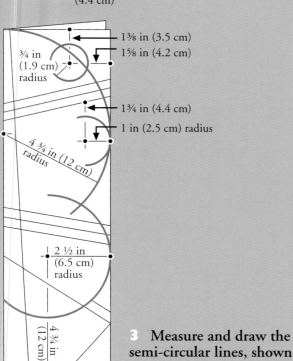

1 ⅜ in (3.5 cm)

1 ⅝ in (4.2 cm)

¾ in (1.9 cm) radius

1 ¾ in (4.4 cm)

1 in (2.5 cm) radius

4 ¾ in (12 cm) radius

2 ½ in (6.5 cm) radius

4 ¾ in (12 cm)

3 Measure and draw the semi-circular lines, shown in red.

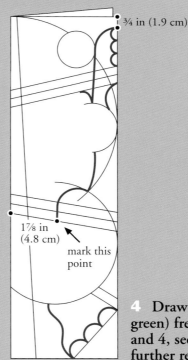

¾ in (1.9 cm)

1 ⅞ in (4.8 cm)

mark this point

4 Draw the lines (shown in green) freehand. For steps 3 and 4, see layout on p 42 for further reference.

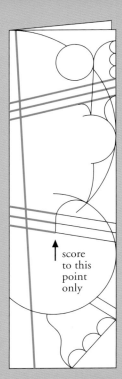

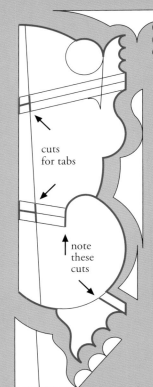

6 Cut along lines, shown in blue. Use a craft knife. Where possible, cut upper and lower sheets together, ensuring symmetry. Unfold.

5 Score the fold lines, shown in red. Make sure that both the top and bottom sheets of paper are sufficiently scored.

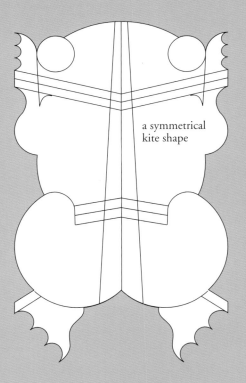

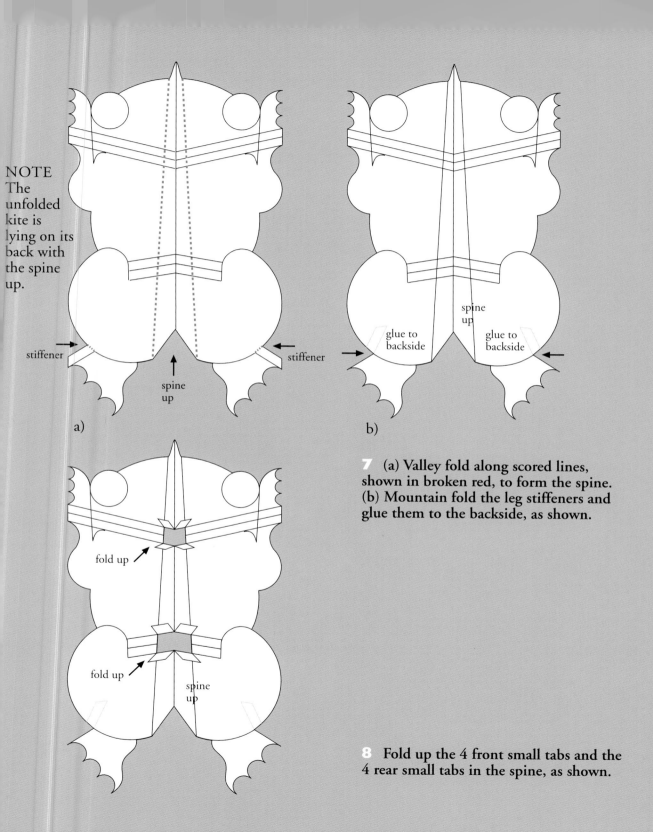

NOTE
The unfolded kite is lying on its back with the spine up.

stiffener

spine up

a)

stiffener

glue to backside

spine up

glue to backside

b)

7 (a) Valley fold along scored lines, shown in broken red, to form the spine. (b) Mountain fold the leg stiffeners and glue them to the backside, as shown.

fold up

fold up

spine up

8 Fold up the 4 front small tabs and the 4 rear small tabs in the spine, as shown.

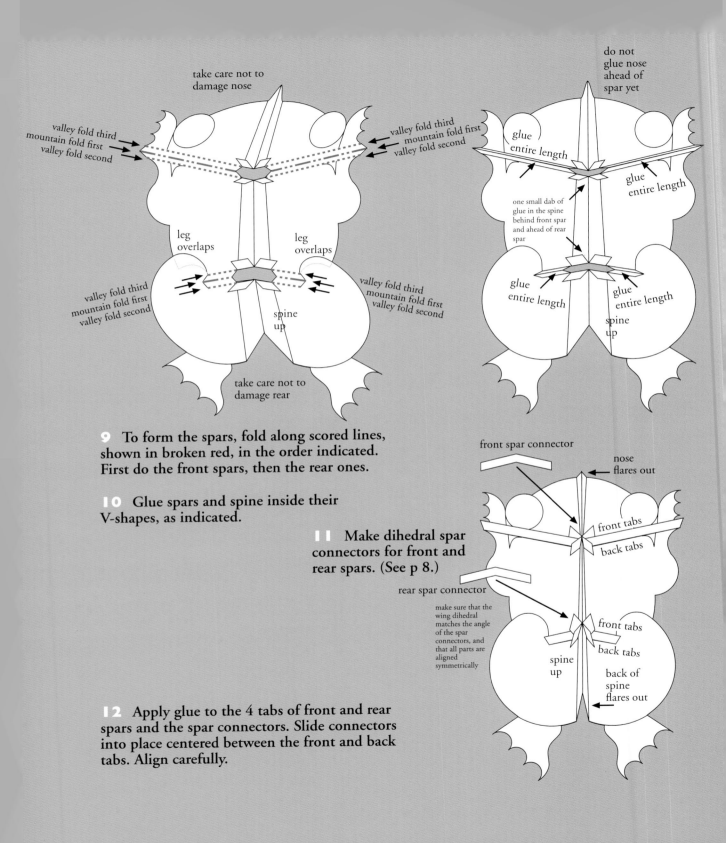

take care not to
damage nose

valley fold third
mountain fold first
valley fold second

valley fold third
mountain fold first
valley fold second

leg
overlaps

leg
overlaps

valley fold third
mountain fold first
valley fold second

valley fold third
mountain fold first
valley fold second

spine
up

take care not to
damage rear

do not
glue nose
ahead of
spar yet

glue
entire length

glue
entire length

one small dab of
glue in the spine
behind front spar
and ahead of rear
spar

glue
entire length

glue
entire length

spine
up

9 To form the spars, fold along scored lines,
shown in broken red, in the order indicated.
First do the front spars, then the rear ones.

10 Glue spars and spine inside their
V-shapes, as indicated.

11 Make dihedral spar
connectors for front and
rear spars. (See p 8.)

front spar connector

nose
flares out

front tabs

back tabs

rear spar connector

make sure that the
wing dihedral
matches the angle
of the spar
connectors, and
that all parts are
aligned
symmetrically

front tabs

back tabs

spine
up

back of
spine
flares out

12 Apply glue to the 4 tabs of front and rear
spars and the spar connectors. Slide connectors
into place centered between the front and back
tabs. Align carefully.

glue tip
of nose
only

13 Press the junction of spars and spine firmly together and hold (or clamp) until glue has set. When all other glue is completely dry, glue the tip of the nose.

spine
up

back of spine
flares out

view of kite in flight

no concave here   no concave here

tail attaches
at the back
of spine

14 For best results, the kite should be adjusted as indicated. Make sure all glue is completely dry before flying kite.

the towing point, where the flying line attaches, is about ½ in (1.25 cm) behind the junction of spars and spine

THUNDERBIRD

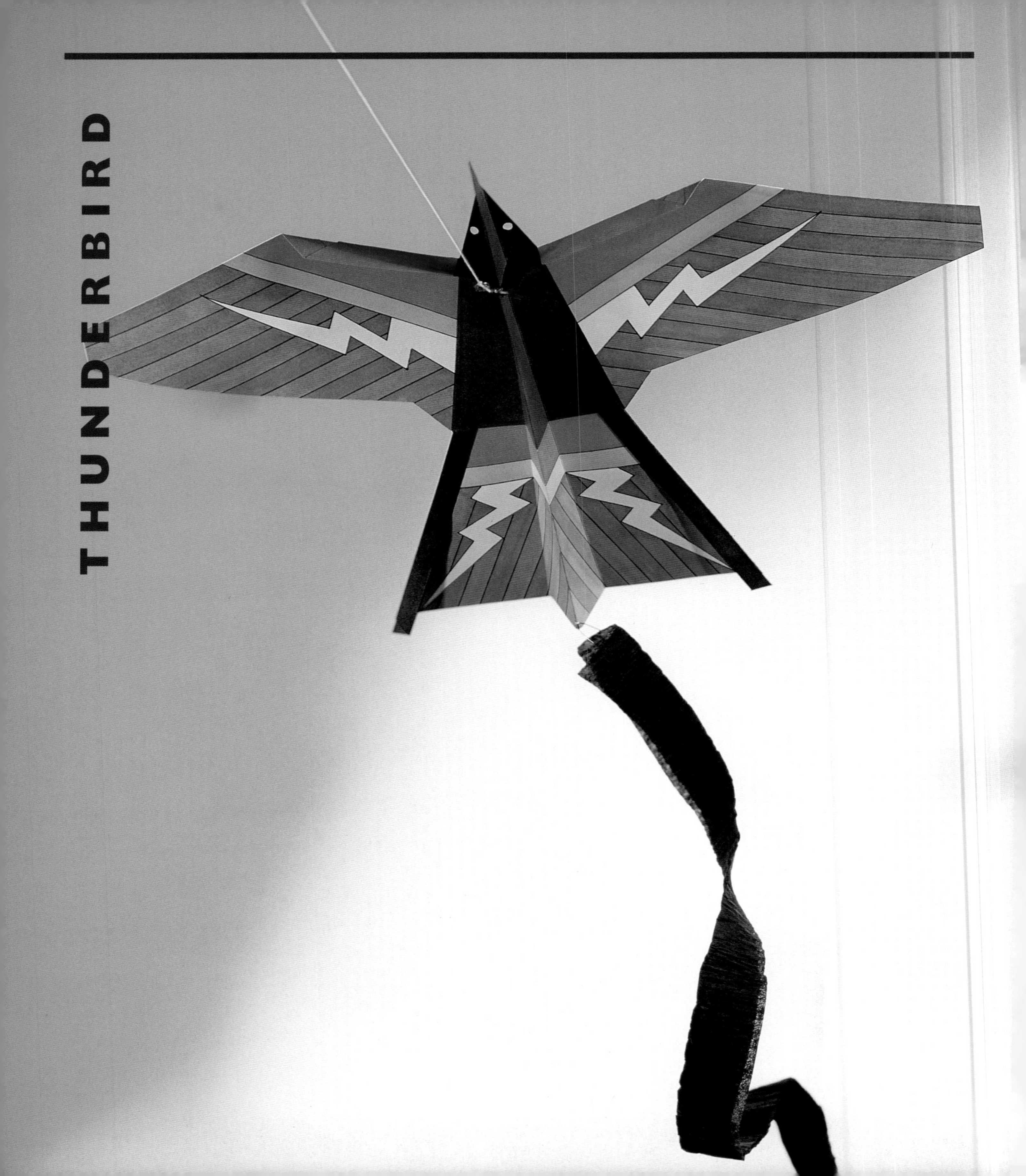

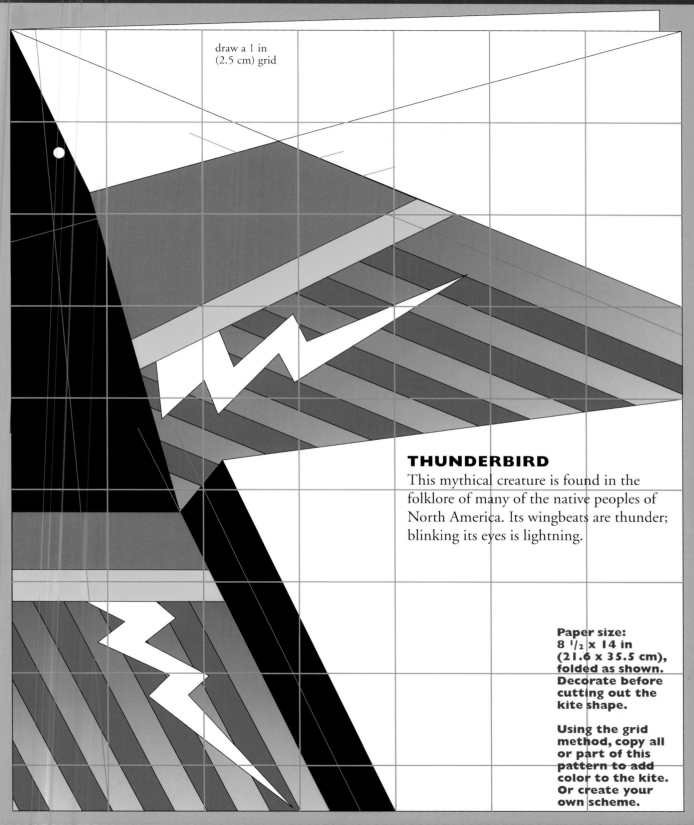

draw a 1 in
(2.5 cm) grid

THUNDERBIRD

This mythical creature is found in the folklore of many of the native peoples of North America. Its wingbeats are thunder; blinking its eyes is lightning.

**Paper size:
8 ¹/₂ x 14 in
(21.6 x 35.5 cm),
folded as shown.
Decorate before
cutting out the
kite shape.**

**Using the grid
method, copy all
or part of this
pattern to add
color to the kite.
Or create your
own scheme.**

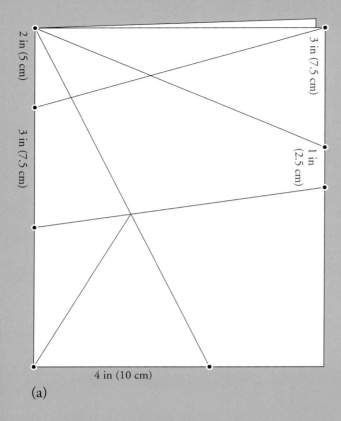

2 in (5 cm)

3 in (7.5 cm)

3 in (7.5 cm)

1 in (2.5 cm)

4 in (10 cm)

(a)

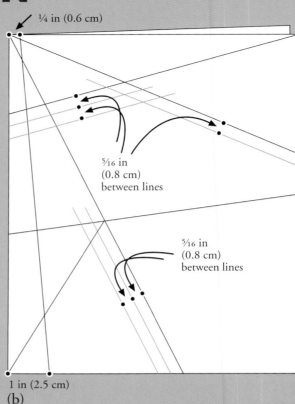

¼ in (0.6 cm)

5⁄16 in (0.8 cm) between lines

5⁄16 in (0.8 cm) between lines

1 in (2.5 cm)

(b)

1 Paper size: 8 ½ x 14 in (21.6 x 35.5 cm). (a) Lay paper flat in a horizontal direction. Valley fold in half vertically. Measure and draw the basic lines. (b) Measure and draw fold lines, shown in orange.

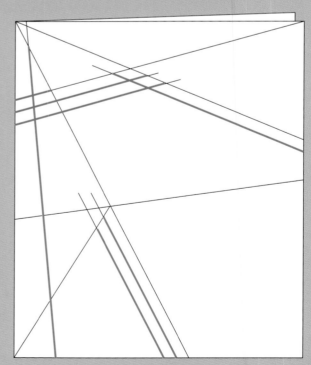

2 Score the fold lines, shown in red. Make sure that both the top and bottom sheets of paper are sufficiently scored.

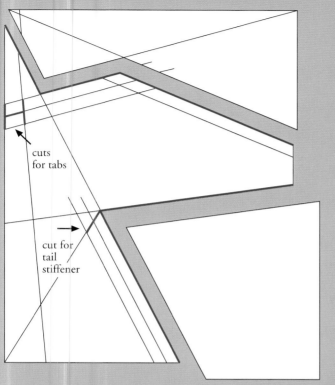

cuts
for tabs

cut for
tail
stiffener

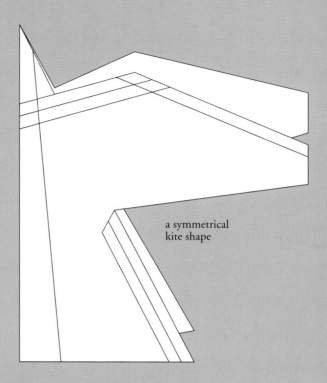

a symmetrical
kite shape

3 Cut along lines shown in blue. Use a craft knife. Where possible, cut upper and lower sheets together, ensuring symmetry. Unfold.

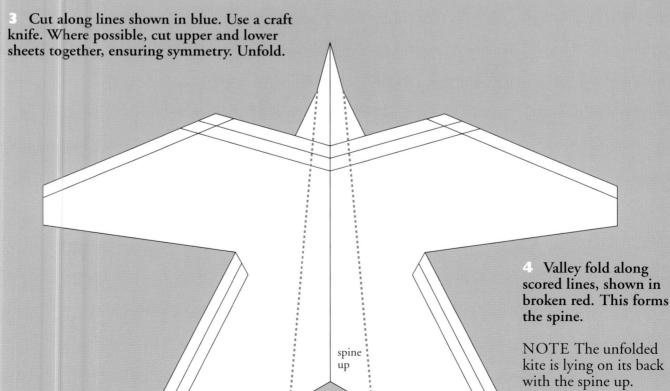

spine
up

4 Valley fold along scored lines, shown in broken red. This forms the spine.

NOTE The unfolded kite is lying on its back with the spine up.

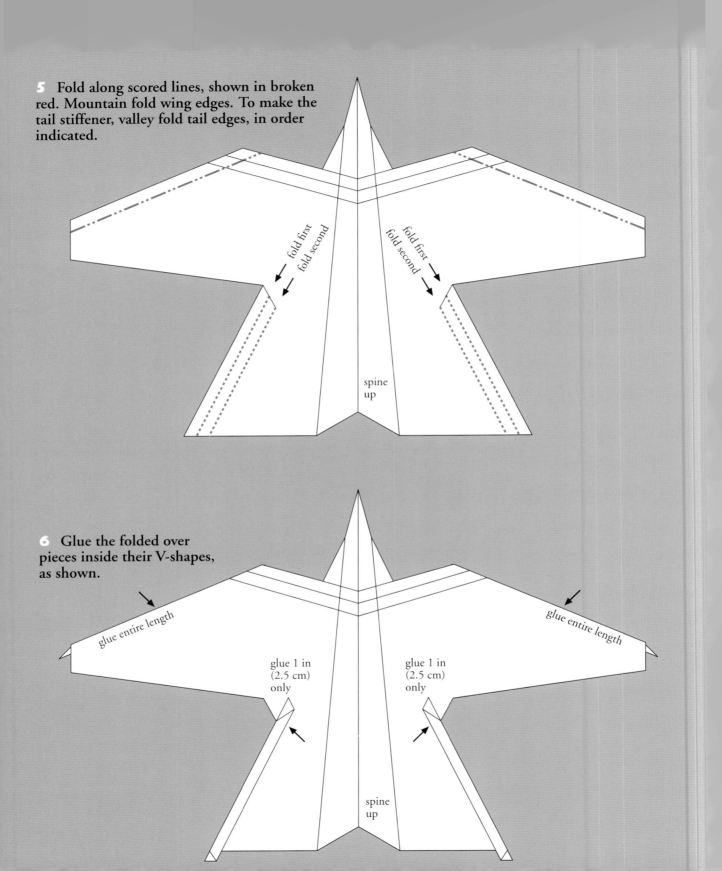

5 Fold along scored lines, shown in broken red. Mountain fold wing edges. To make the tail stiffener, valley fold tail edges, in order indicated.

fold first
fold second

fold first
fold second

spine up

6 Glue the folded over pieces inside their V-shapes, as shown.

glue entire length

glue entire length

glue 1 in (2.5 cm) only

glue 1 in (2.5 cm) only

spine up

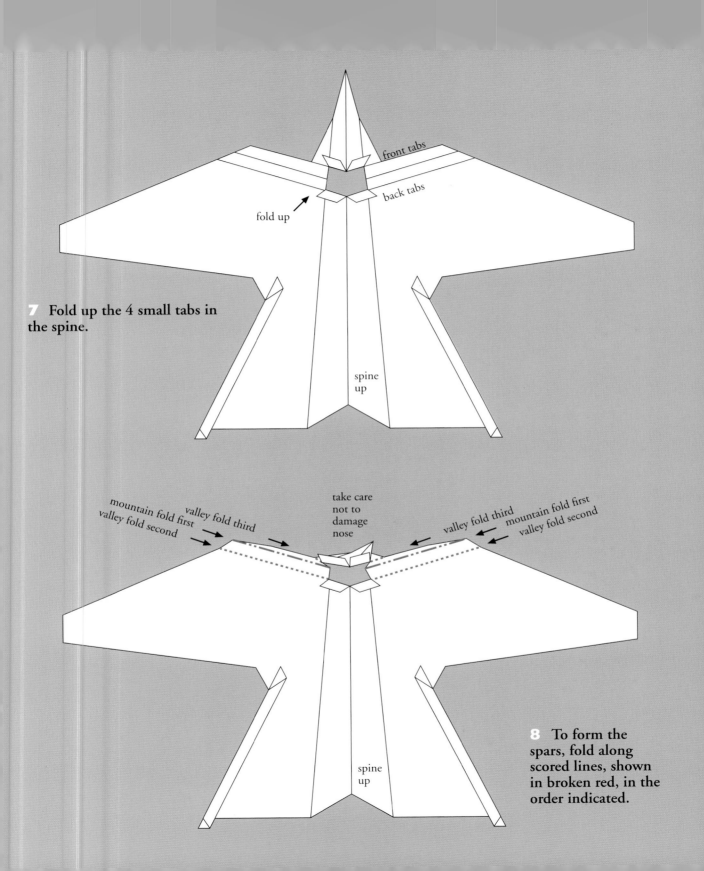

7 Fold up the 4 small tabs in the spine.

front tabs

back tabs

fold up

spine up

mountain fold first
valley fold second
valley fold third

take care not to damage nose

valley fold third
mountain fold first
valley fold second

spine up

8 To form the spars, fold along scored lines, shown in broken red, in the order indicated.

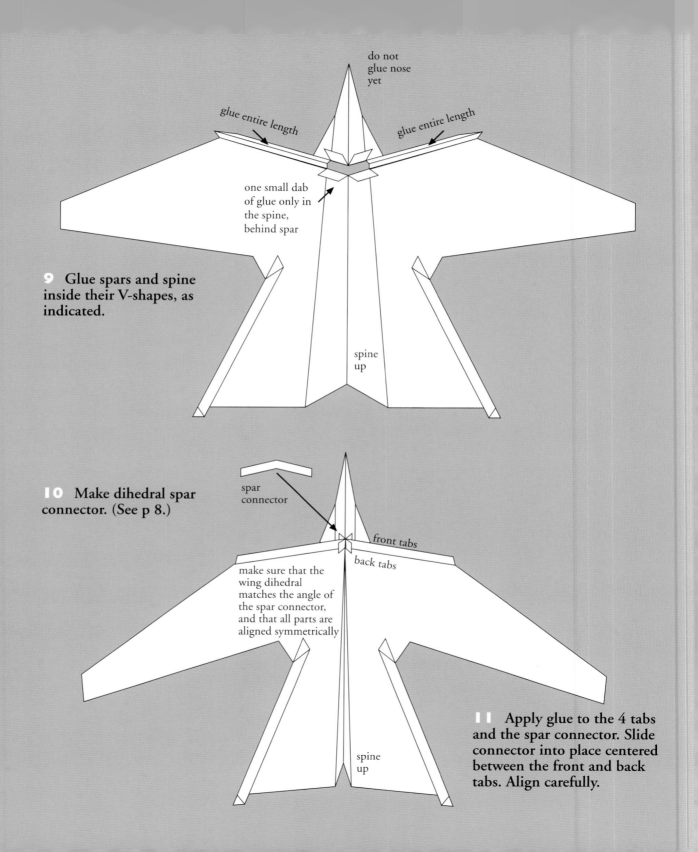

do not
glue nose
yet

glue entire length

glue entire length

one small dab
of glue only in
the spine,
behind spar

9 Glue spars and spine inside their V-shapes, as indicated.

spine
up

10 Make dihedral spar connector. (See p 8.)

spar
connector

front tabs

back tabs

make sure that the
wing dihedral
matches the angle of
the spar connector,
and that all parts are
aligned symmetrically

spine
up

11 Apply glue to the 4 tabs and the spar connector. Slide connector into place centered between the front and back tabs. Align carefully.

12 Press the junction of spars and spine firmly together and hold (or clamp) until glue has set. When all other glue is completely dry, glue the tip of the nose.

glue tip of nose only

13 For best results, the kite should be adjusted as indicated. Make sure all glue is completely dry before flying kite.

spine up

back of spine flares out

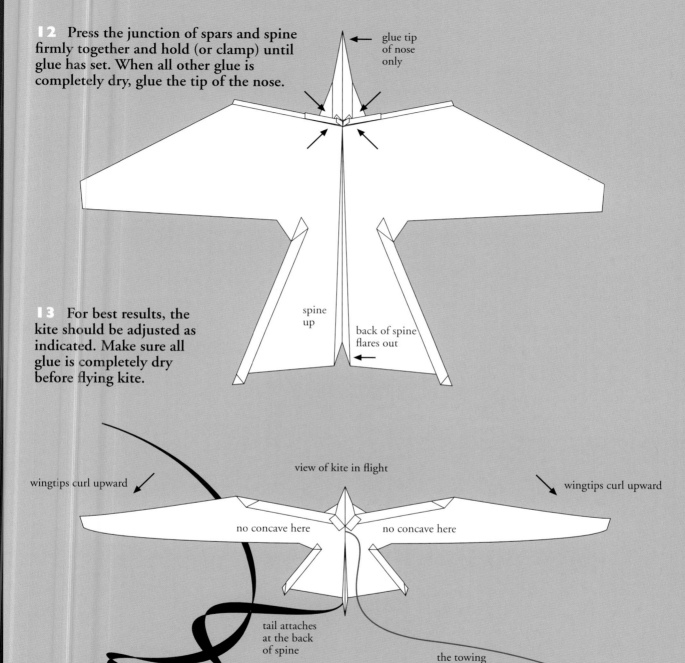

view of kite in flight

wingtips curl upward

no concave here

no concave here

wingtips curl upward

tail attaches at the back of spine

the towing point, where the flying line attaches, is just behind the junction of spars and spine

55

PHOENIX

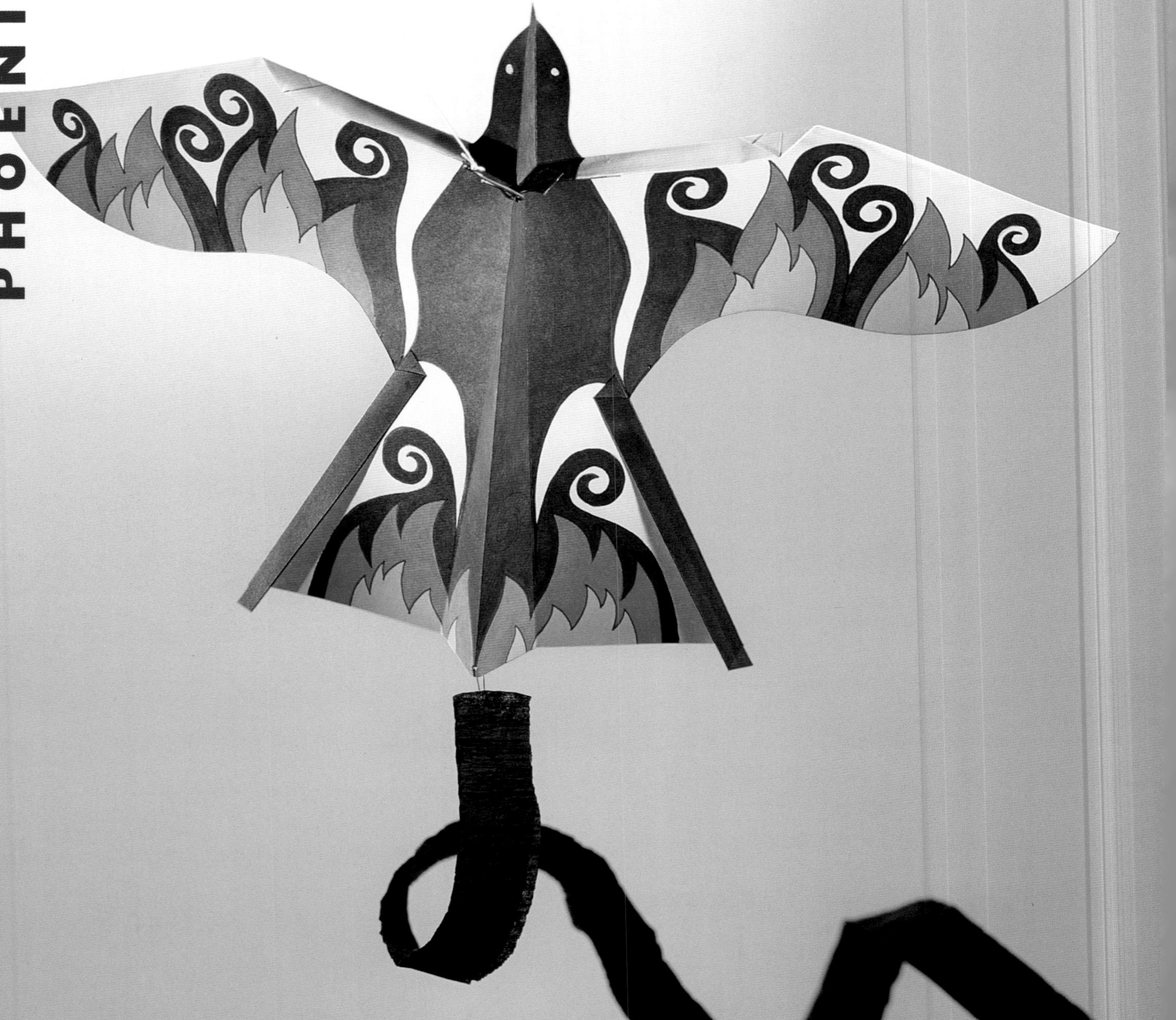

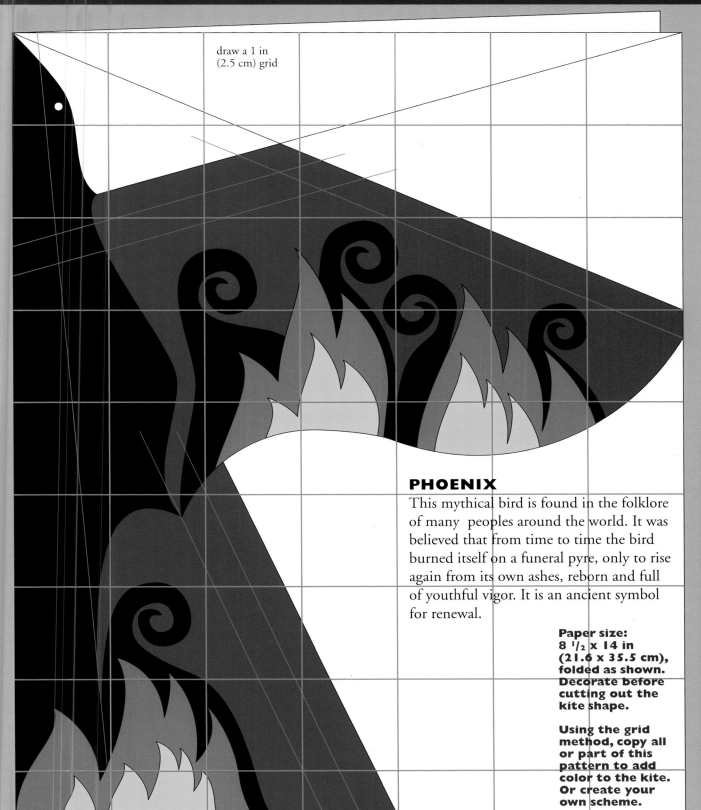

draw a 1 in
(2.5 cm) grid

PHOENIX

PHOENIX

This mythical bird is found in the folklore of many peoples around the world. It was believed that from time to time the bird burned itself on a funeral pyre, only to rise again from its own ashes, reborn and full of youthful vigor. It is an ancient symbol for renewal.

**Paper size:
8 ¹/₂ x 14 in
(21.6 x 35.5 cm),
folded as shown.
Decorate before
cutting out the
kite shape.**

**Using the grid
method, copy all
or part of this
pattern to add
color to the kite.
Or create your
own scheme.**

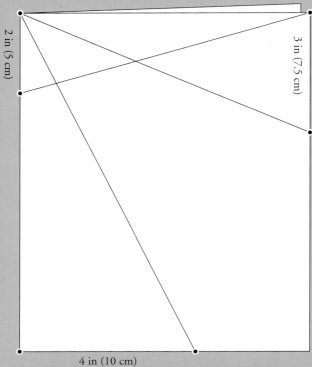

2 in (5 cm)

3 in (7.5 cm)

4 in (10 cm)

(a)

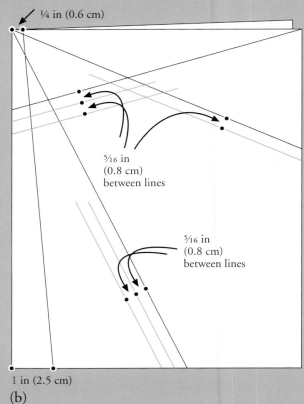

¼ in (0.6 cm)

⁵⁄₁₆ in (0.8 cm) between lines

⁵⁄₁₆ in (0.8 cm) between lines

1 in (2.5 cm)

(b)

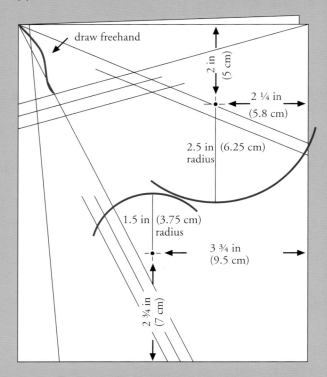

draw freehand

2 in (5 cm)

2 ¼ in (5.8 cm)

2.5 in (6.25 cm) radius

1.5 in (3.75 cm) radius

3 ¾ in (9.5 cm)

2 ¾ in (7 cm)

1 Paper size: 8 ½ x 14 in (21.6 x 35.5 cm). (a) Lay paper flat in a horizontal direction. Valley fold in half vertically. Measure and draw the basic lines. (b) Measure and draw fold lines, shown in orange.

2 Add curved lines, shown in green. Use the layout on p 57 for further reference.

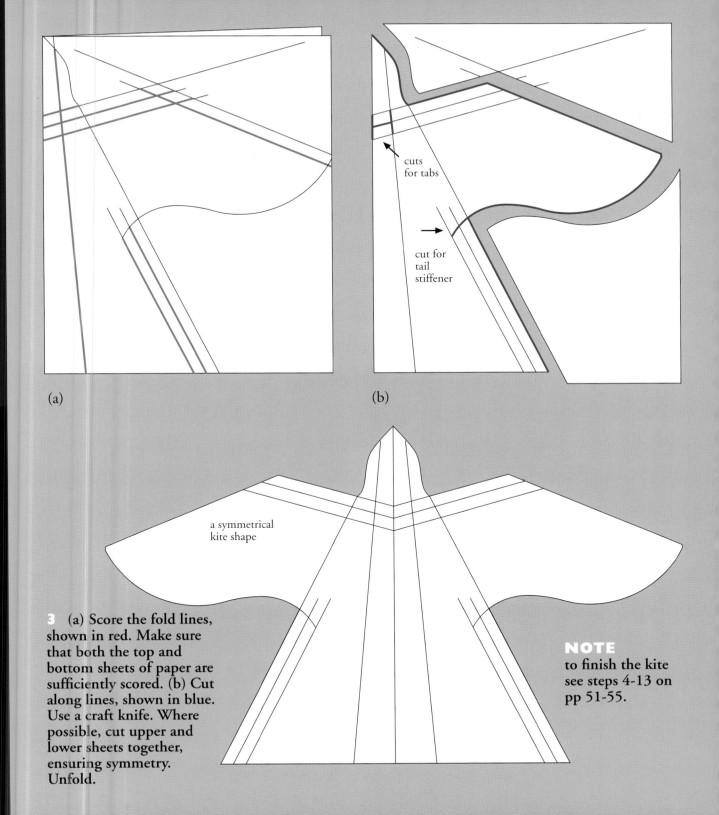

(a)

(b)

cuts
for tabs

cut for
tail
stiffener

a symmetrical
kite shape

3 (a) Score the fold lines, shown in red. Make sure that both the top and bottom sheets of paper are sufficiently scored. (b) Cut along lines, shown in blue. Use a craft knife. Where possible, cut upper and lower sheets together, ensuring symmetry. Unfold.

NOTE
to finish the kite see steps 4-13 on pp 51-55.

SWALLOW

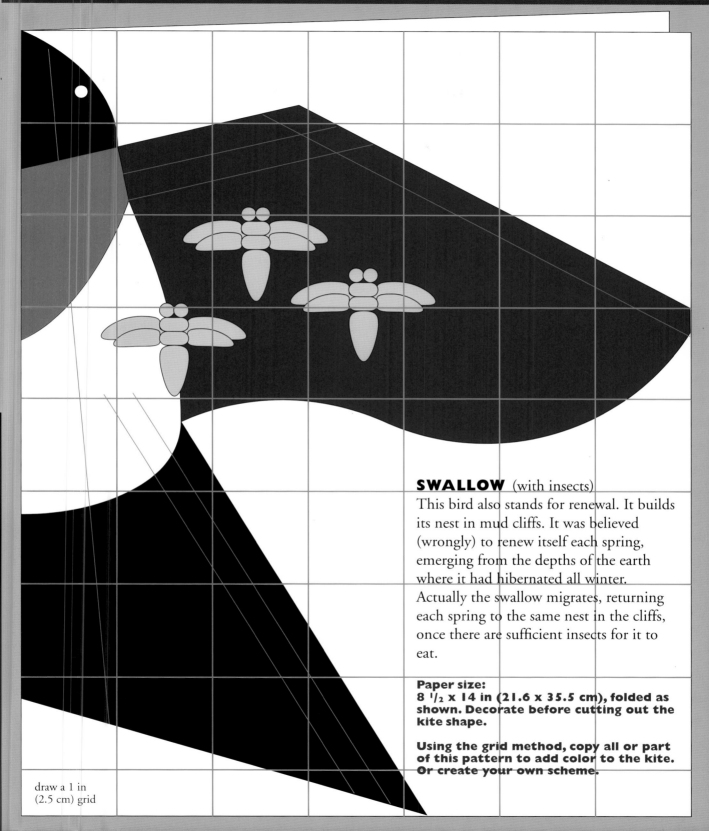

SWALLOW (with insects)

This bird also stands for renewal. It builds its nest in mud cliffs. It was believed (wrongly) to renew itself each spring, emerging from the depths of the earth where it had hibernated all winter.

Actually the swallow migrates, returning each spring to the same nest in the cliffs, once there are sufficient insects for it to eat.

Paper size:
8 ¹/₂ x 14 in (21.6 x 35.5 cm), folded as shown. Decorate before cutting out the kite shape.

Using the grid method, copy all or part of this pattern to add color to the kite. Or create your own scheme.

draw a 1 in
(2.5 cm) grid

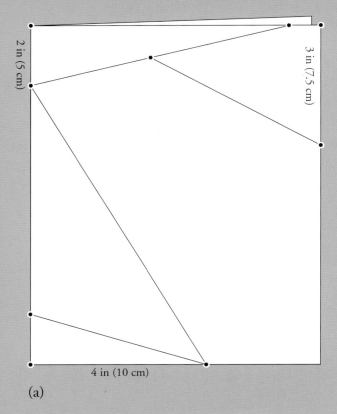

2 in (5 cm)

3 in (7.5 cm)

4 in (10 cm)

(a)

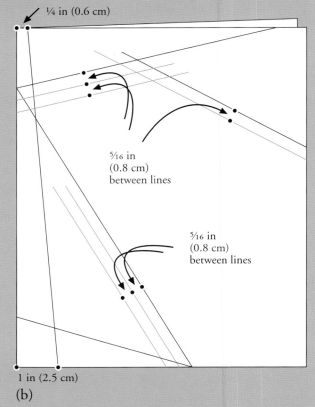

¼ in (0.6 cm)

5⁄16 in (0.8 cm) between lines

5⁄16 in (0.8 cm) between lines

1 in (2.5 cm)

(b)

1 Paper size: 8 ½ x 14 in (21.6 x 35.5 cm). (a) Lay paper flat in a horizontal direction. Valley fold in half vertically. Measure and draw the basic lines. (b) Measure and draw fold lines, shown in orange.

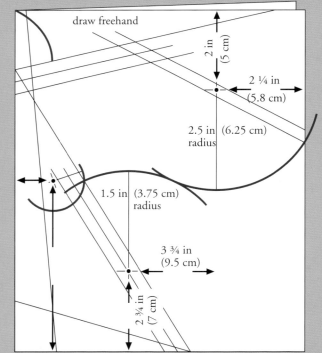

draw freehand

2 in (5 cm)

2 ¼ in (5.8 cm)

2.5 in (6.25 cm) radius

1.5 in (3.75 cm) radius

3 ¾ in (9.5 cm)

2 ¾ in (7 cm)

2 Add curved lines, shown in green. Use the layout on p 61 for further reference.

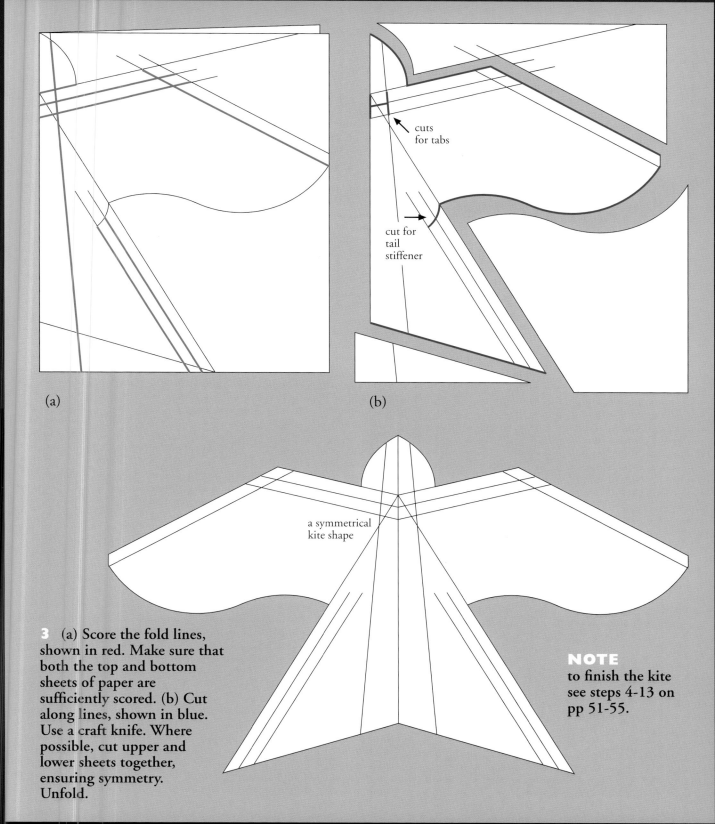

(a)

(b)

cuts
for tabs

cut for
tail
stiffener

a symmetrical
kite shape

3 (a) Score the fold lines, shown in red. Make sure that both the top and bottom sheets of paper are sufficiently scored. (b) Cut along lines, shown in blue. Use a craft knife. Where possible, cut upper and lower sheets together, ensuring symmetry. Unfold.

NOTE
to finish the kite see steps 4-13 on pp 51-55.

GOLDFINCH (with thistles)
The goldfinch likes to eat the seeds of thistles and thorns of all kinds. Because these plants represent hardship, this bird stands for well-being and joy in the midst of suffering. Therefore in the Christian religion it represents the passion of Christ. In addition to this, the goldfinch demonstrates happiness whenever it appears overhead, because it always sings on the wing.

draw a 1 in
(2.5 cm) grid

**Paper size:
8 ¹/₂ x 7 in
(21.6 x 17.75 cm),
folded as shown.
Decorate before
cutting out the
kite shape.**

**Using the grid
method, copy all
or part of this
pattern to add
color to the kite.
Or create your
own scheme.**

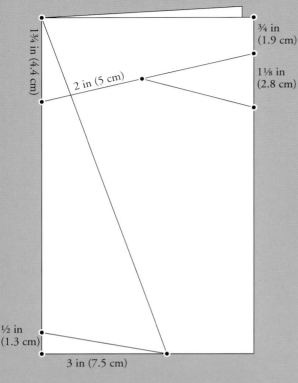

(a)

¾ in (1.9 cm)

1¾ in (4.4 cm)

2 in (5 cm)

1⅛ in (2.8 cm)

½ in (1.3 cm)

3 in (7.5 cm)

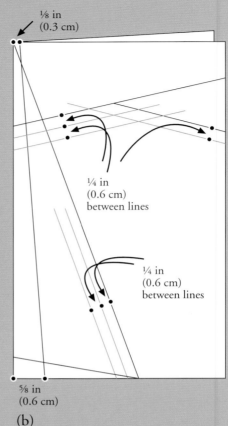

(b)

⅛ in (0.3 cm)

¼ in (0.6 cm) between lines

¼ in (0.6 cm) between lines

⅝ in (0.6 cm)

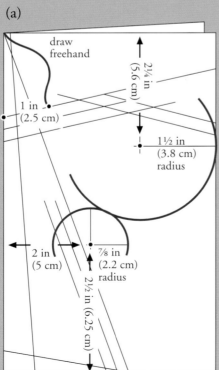

draw freehand

2¼ in (5.6 cm)

1 in (2.5 cm)

1½ in (3.8 cm) radius

2 in (5 cm)

⅞ in (2.2 cm) radius

2½ in (6.25 cm)

1 Paper size: 8 ½ x 7 in (21.6 x 17.75 cm). (a) Lay paper flat in a horizontal direction. Valley fold in half vertically. Measure and draw the basic lines. (b) Measure and draw fold lines, shown in orange.

2 Add curved lines, shown in green. Use the layout on p 65 for further reference.

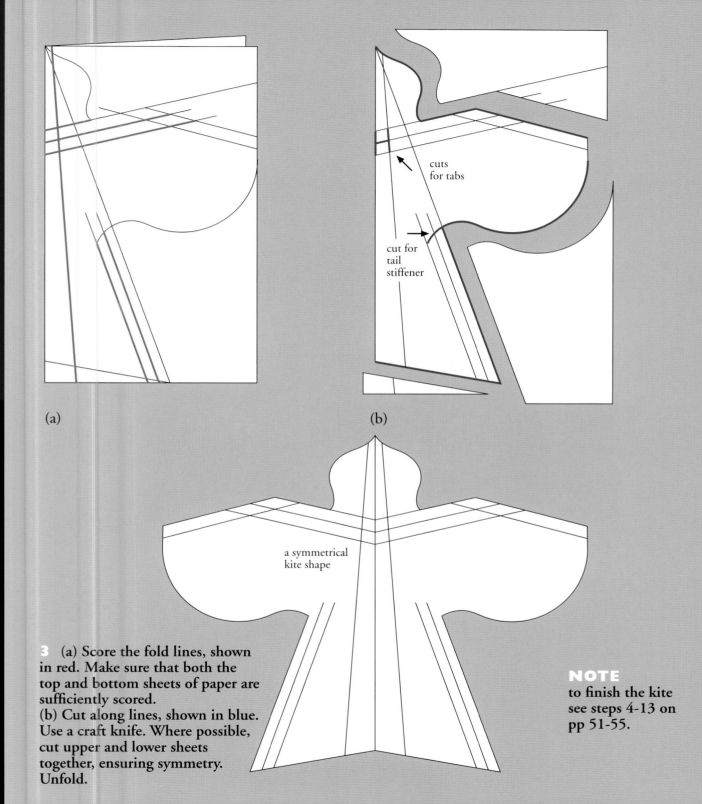

(a)

(b)

cuts
for tabs

cut for
tail
stiffener

a symmetrical
kite shape

3 (a) Score the fold lines, shown
in red. Make sure that both the
top and bottom sheets of paper are
sufficiently scored.
(b) Cut along lines, shown in blue.
Use a craft knife. Where possible,
cut upper and lower sheets
together, ensuring symmetry.
Unfold.

NOTE

to finish the kite
see steps 4-13 on
pp 51-55.

DRAGONFLY

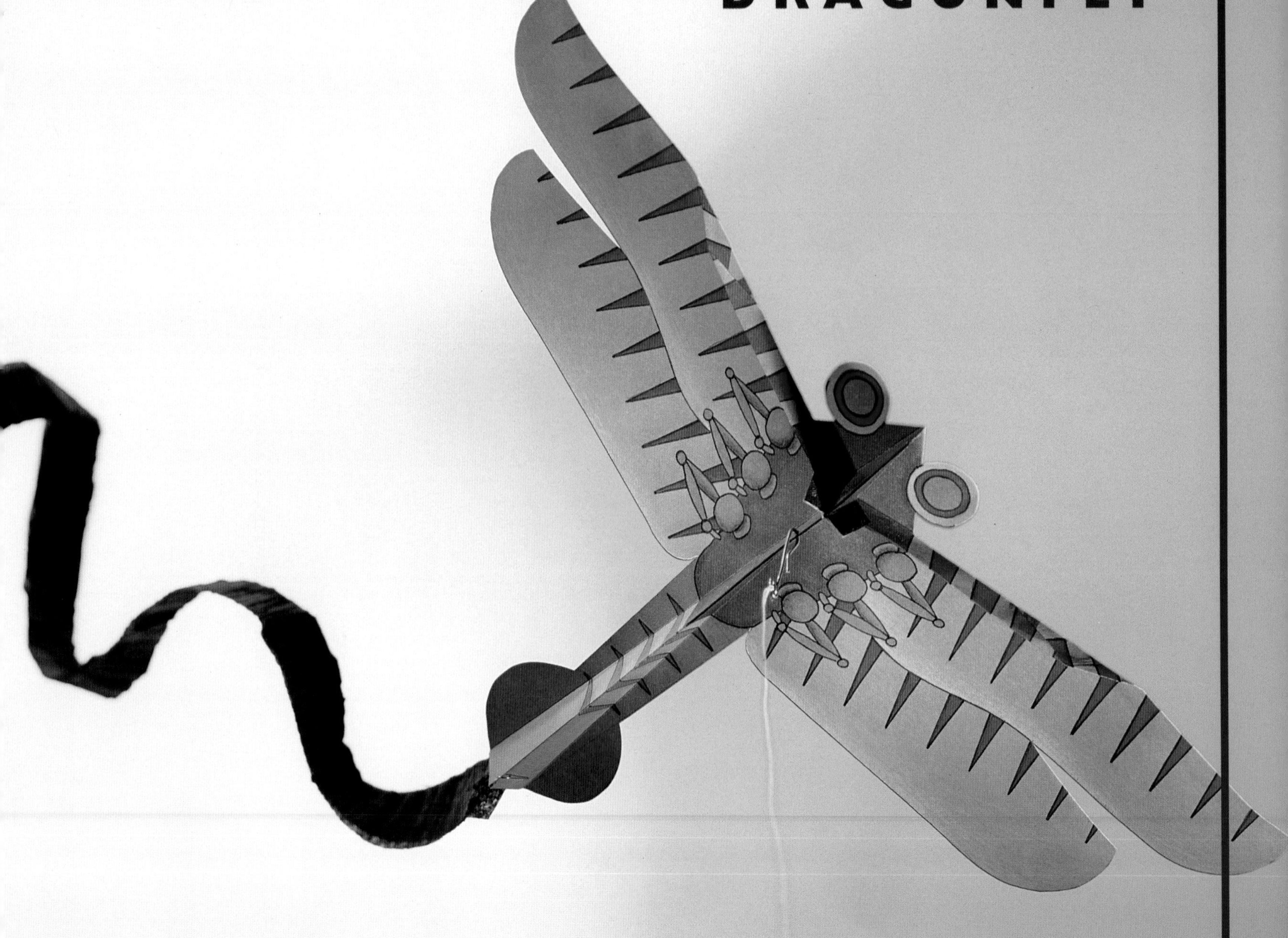

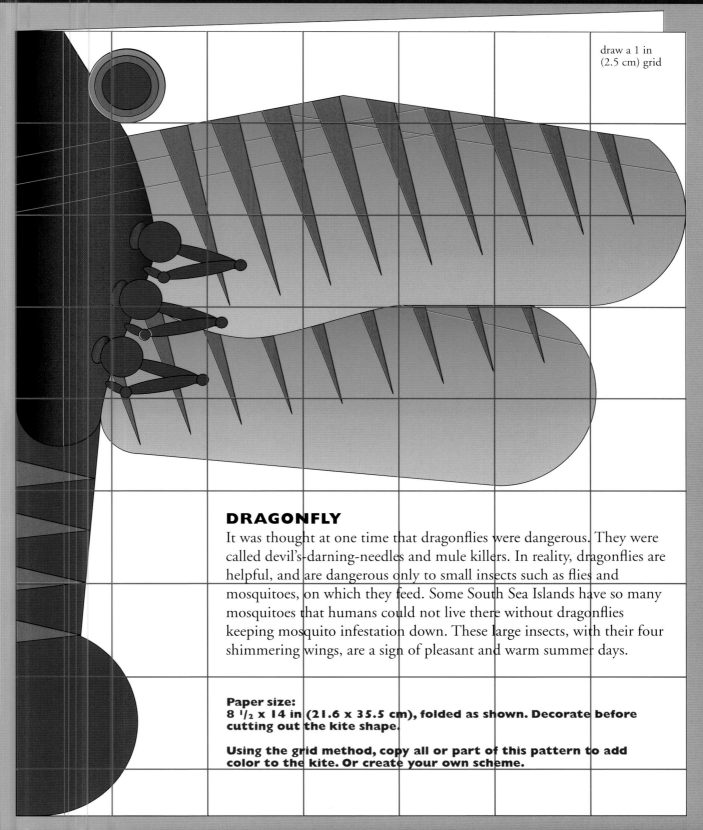

draw a 1 in
(2.5 cm) grid

DRAGONFLY

It was thought at one time that dragonflies were dangerous. They were called devil's-darning-needles and mule killers. In reality, dragonflies are helpful, and are dangerous only to small insects such as flies and mosquitoes, on which they feed. Some South Sea Islands have so many mosquitoes that humans could not live there without dragonflies keeping mosquito infestation down. These large insects, with their four shimmering wings, are a sign of pleasant and warm summer days.

Paper size:
8 ¹/₂ x 14 in (21.6 x 35.5 cm), folded as shown. Decorate before cutting out the kite shape.

Using the grid method, copy all or part of this pattern to add color to the kite. Or create your own scheme.

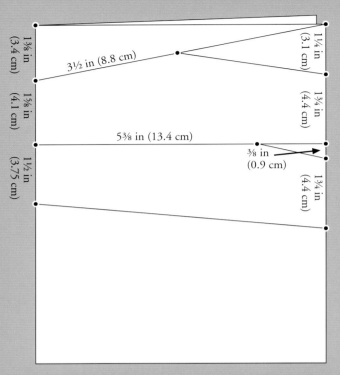

1⅜ in (3.4 cm)

1⅝ in (4.1 cm)

1½ in (3.75 cm)

3½ in (8.8 cm)

1¼ in (3.1 cm)

1¾ in (4.4 cm)

5⅜ in (13.4 cm)

⅜ in (0.9 cm)

1¾ in (4.4 cm)

(a)

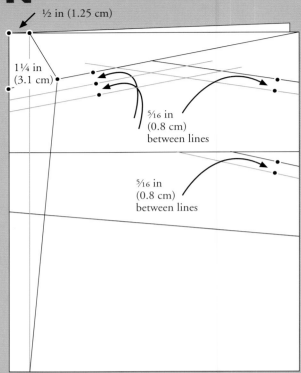

½ in (1.25 cm)

1¼ in (3.1 cm)

5/16 in (0.8 cm) between lines

5/16 in (0.8 cm) between lines

(b)

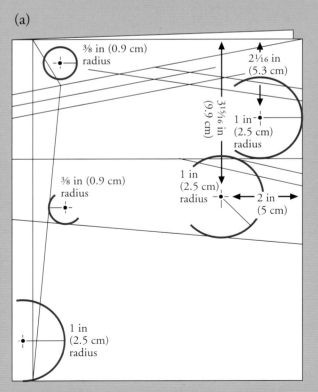

⅜ in (0.9 cm) radius

2 1/16 in (5.3 cm)

3 15/16 in (9.9 cm)

1 in (2.5 cm) radius

⅜ in (0.9 cm) radius

1 in (2.5 cm) radius

2 in (5 cm)

1 in (2.5 cm) radius

1 Paper size: 8 ½ x 14 in (21.6 x 35.5 cm).
(a) Lay paper flat in a horizontal direction.
Valley fold in half vertically. Measure and draw
the basic lines. (b) Measure and draw fold
lines, shown in orange.

2 Add curved lines, shown in green. Use the
layout on p 69 for further reference.

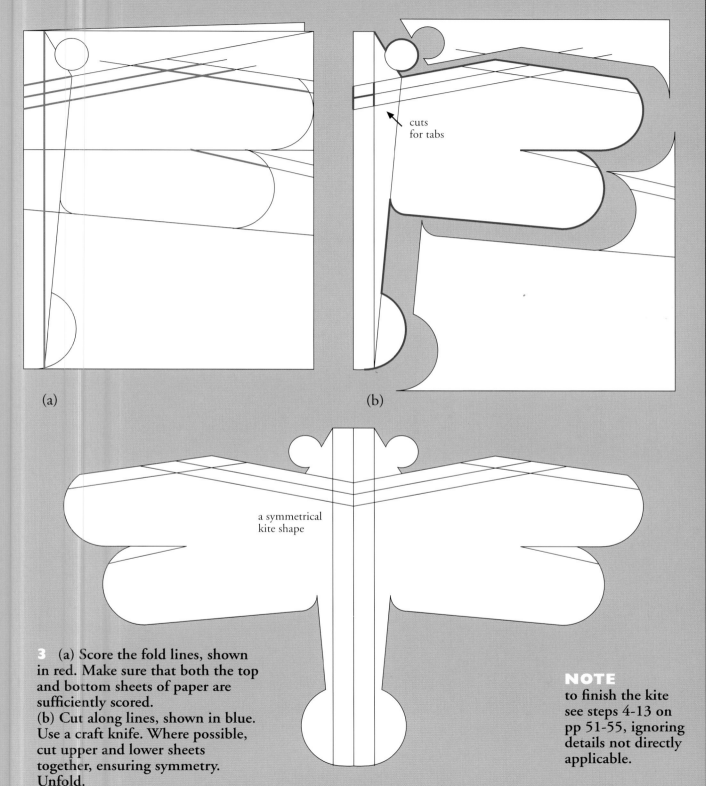

(a)

(b)

cuts
for tabs

a symmetrical
kite shape

3 (a) Score the fold lines, shown
in red. Make sure that both the top
and bottom sheets of paper are
sufficiently scored.
(b) Cut along lines, shown in blue.
Use a craft knife. Where possible,
cut upper and lower sheets
together, ensuring symmetry.
Unfold.

NOTE
to finish the kite
see steps 4-13 on
pp 51-55, ignoring
details not directly
applicable.

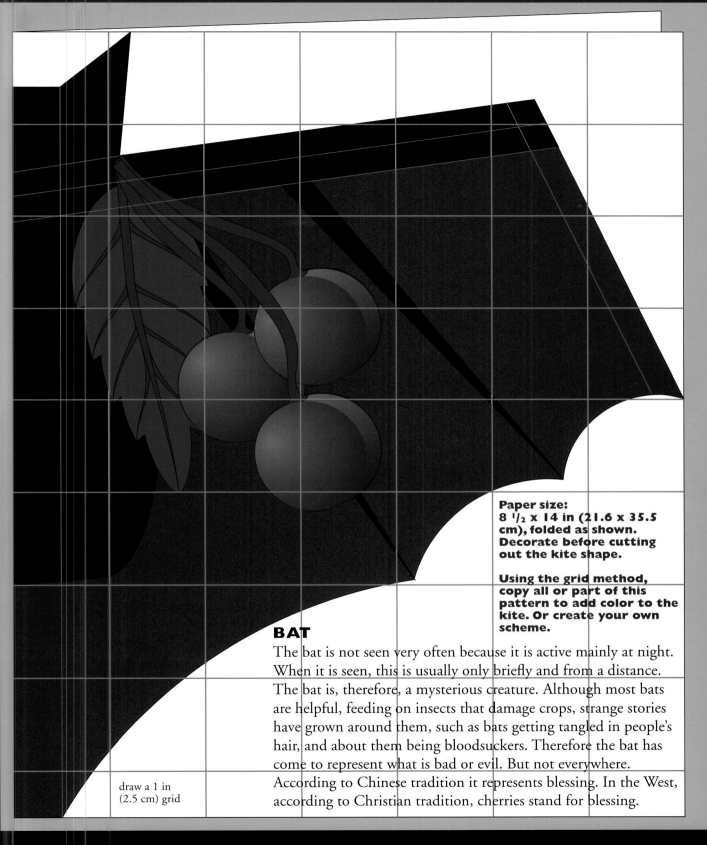

Paper size:
8 ¹/₂ x 14 in (21.6 x 35.5
cm), folded as shown.
Decorate before cutting
out the kite shape.

Using the grid method,
copy all or part of this
pattern to add color to the
kite. Or create your own
scheme.

draw a 1 in
(2.5 cm) grid

BAT

The bat is not seen very often because it is active mainly at night. When it is seen, this is usually only briefly and from a distance. The bat is, therefore, a mysterious creature. Although most bats are helpful, feeding on insects that damage crops, strange stories have grown around them, such as bats getting tangled in people's hair, and about them being bloodsuckers. Therefore the bat has come to represent what is bad or evil. But not everywhere. According to Chinese tradition it represents blessing. In the West, according to Christian tradition, cherries stand for blessing.

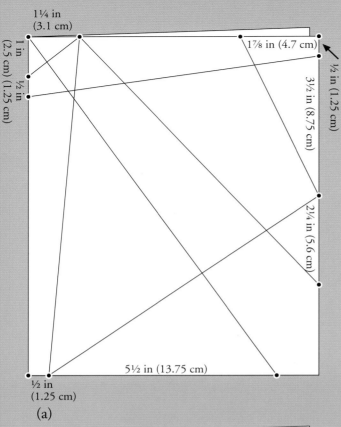

1¼ in (3.1 cm)

1 in (2.5 cm)

½ in (1.25 cm)

1⅞ in (4.7 cm)

½ in (1.25 cm)

3½ in (8.75 cm)

2¼ in (5.6 cm)

5½ in (13.75 cm)

½ in (1.25 cm)

(a)

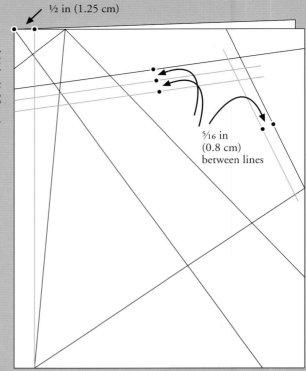

½ in (1.25 cm)

5/16 in (0.8 cm) between lines

(b)

1 Paper size: 8 ½ x 14 in (21.6 x 35.5 cm). (a) Lay paper flat in a horizontal direction. Valley fold in half vertically. Measure and draw the basic lines. (b) Measure and draw fold lines, shown in orange.

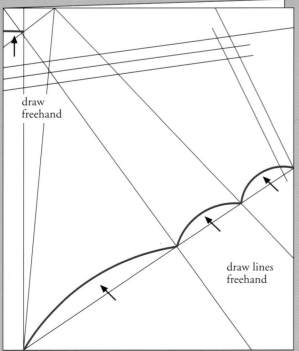

draw freehand

draw lines freehand

2 Add details to head and wings, shown in green. Draw them freehand. Use the layout on p 73 for further reference.

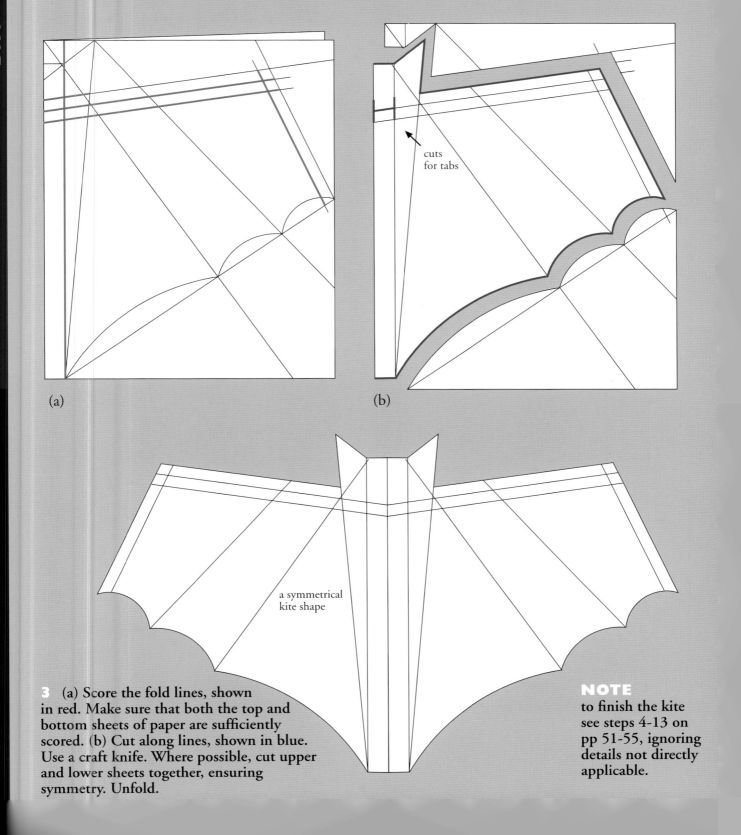

(a)

(b)

cuts
for tabs

a symmetrical
kite shape

3 (a) Score the fold lines, shown
in red. Make sure that both the top and
bottom sheets of paper are sufficiently
scored. (b) Cut along lines, shown in blue.
Use a craft knife. Where possible, cut upper
and lower sheets together, ensuring
symmetry. Unfold.

NOTE
to finish the kite
see steps 4-13 on
pp 51-55, ignoring
details not directly
applicable.

CICADA

draw a 1 in
(2.5 cm) grid

CICADA

The cicada, also called the harvest fly, represents abundance. This creature is found in the warmer regions of the world. It spends most of its life underground in the nymph stage grubbing on roots, some for as long as 17 years. When it finally emerges as an adult, the male cicada sings almost nonstop until it dies, in a few weeks time. Sound is made by rubbing shell-like abdominal membranes together. Cicadas emerge in late summer when harvest time is approaching, often en masse, and the continuous buzzing sound that fills the air is seen as a sign of a bountiful harvest.

**Paper size:
8 ¹/₂ x 11 in (21.6 x 28 cm),
folded as shown. Decorate
before cutting out the kite
shape.**

**Using the grid method,
copy all or part of this
pattern to add color to the
kite. Or create your own
scheme.**

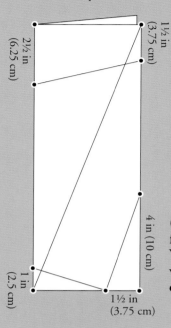

2½ in (6.25 cm)

1½ in (3.75 cm)

1 in (2.5 cm)

4 in (10 cm)

1½ in (3.75 cm)

1 Paper size: 8 ½ x 11 in (21.6 x 28 cm). Lay paper flat in a vertical direction. Valley fold in half vertically. Measure and draw the basic lines.

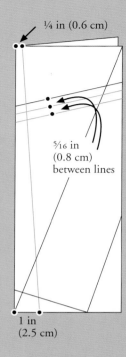

¼ in (0.6 cm)

⁵⁄₁₆ in (0.8 cm) between lines

1 in (2.5 cm)

2 Measure and draw the fold lines.

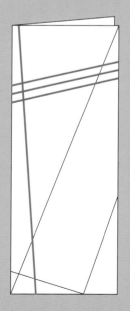

3 Score the fold lines, shown in red. Make sure that both the top and bottom sheets of paper are sufficiently scored.

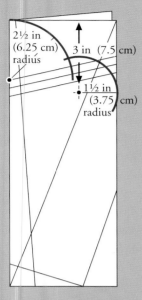

4 First add curved line, shown in red. Then add another curved line (shown in green) drawn freehand, using the reference point.

2½ in (6.25 cm) radius

3 in (7.5 cm)

1½ in (3.75 cm) radius

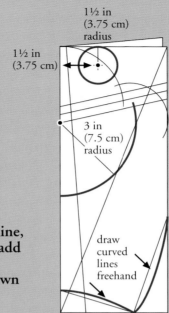

5 Measure and add the stem line (shown in green). The leaf sawtooth edge (also shown in green) is drawn freehand, as indicated.

1½ in (3.75 cm) radius

1½ in (3.75 cm)

3 in (7.5 cm) radius

draw curved lines freehand

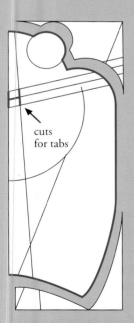

cuts for tabs

6 Cut along lines, shown in blue. Use a craft knife. Where possible, cut upper and lower sheets together, ensuring symmetry. Unfold.

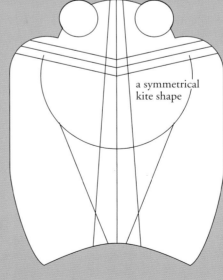

a symmetrical kite shape

NOTE
to finish the kite see steps 4-11 on pp 16-19.

PAINTED LADY

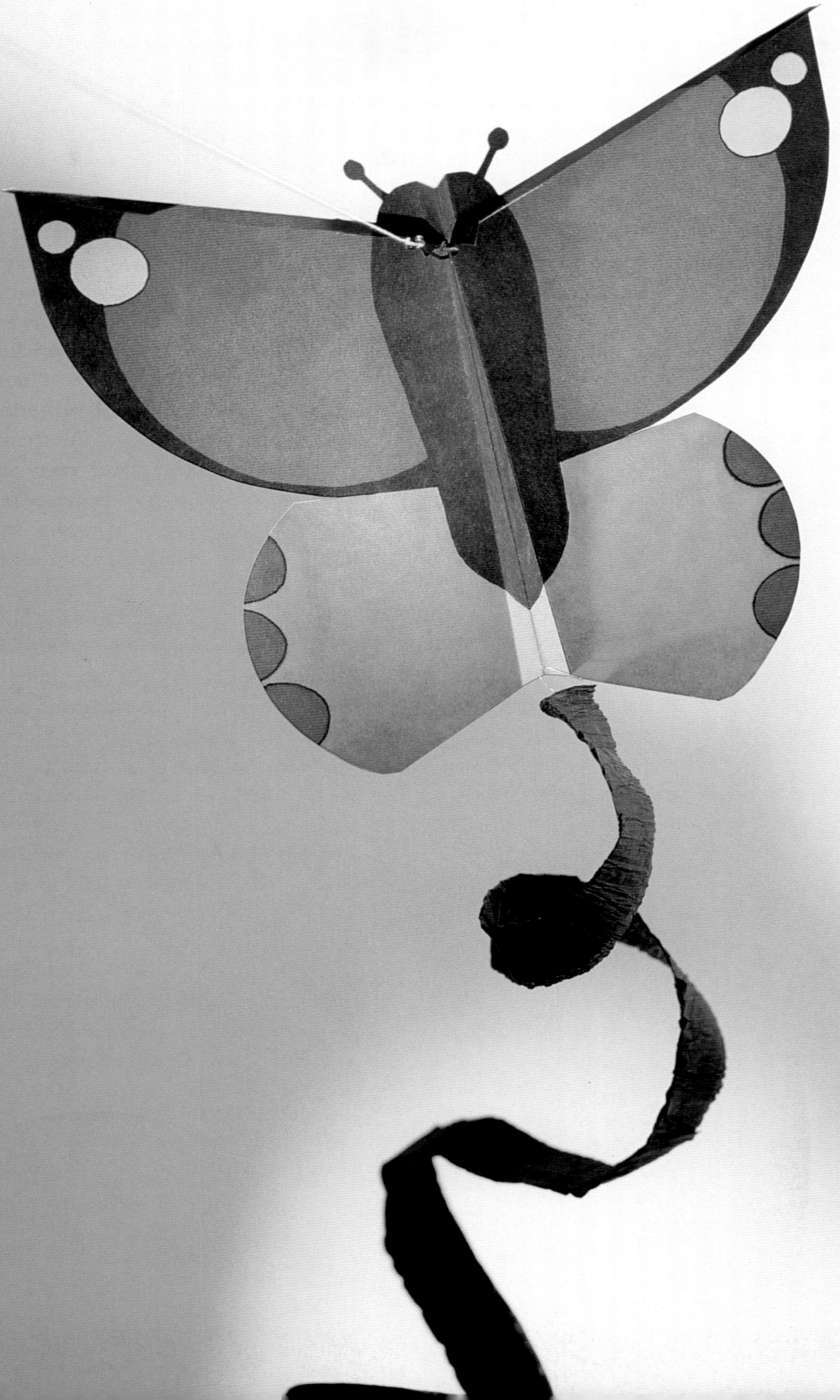

decoration

draw a 1 in
(2.5 cm) grid

Paper size:
8 ¹/₂ x 7 in (21.6 x 17.75 cm), folded as shown. Decorate
before cutting out the kite shape.

**Using the grid method, copy all or part of this pattern to
add color to the kite. Or create your own scheme.**

PAINTED LADY

The Painted Lady is the most widely
distributed butterfly in the world. Because of
the way in which their life develops,
butterflies represent eternal hope or eternal
life. Butterflies develop through four unique
stages, during each one they look different
and live in a completely new way. The adult
lays eggs, and the worm-like hatchlings that
emerge grow into beautiful caterpillars. The
caterpillars of various kinds of butterflies are
quite different, some have horns, spines, or
hair, some are striped or mottled in color,
but none resemble the adult butterfly each
will someday become. Caterpillars eat an
enormous amount as they grow. The Painted
Lady is so widely distributed because its
caterpillar feeds on weedy plants such as
burdocks, nettles, and thistles, which grow
everywhere. Caterpillars shed their skin four
or five times before they are fully grown.
When mature, a caterpillar spins a small silk
button on a twig or other object, and as it
sheds its skin for the last time, it attaches
one end of its body to the button and forms
a hard outer shell. Some shells have strange
shapes. Many have brightly colored patterns.
Often they glisten in gold or silver hues,
which has given this stage the name of
chrysalis (meaning gold in Greek). The
chrysalis does not eat or move about, but
uses the food energy the caterpillar stored up
to quietly turn into a completely new
creature – a butterfly – neatly folded inside
the hard shell. When the chrysalis shell
cracks, and the sun dries the wet folded-up
butterfly, and blood begins to flow in its
veins, its wings fan out into a brilliantly
colored, full grown adult, and the cycle starts
over again.

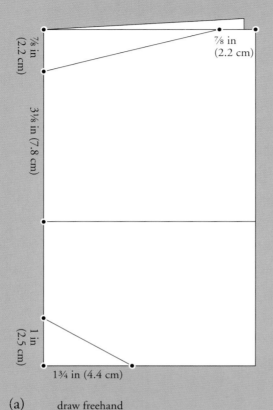

7/8 in (2.2 cm)

3⅛ in (7.8 cm)

7/8 in (2.2 cm)

1 in (2.5 cm)

1¾ in (4.4 cm)

(a)

⅜ in (0.9 cm)

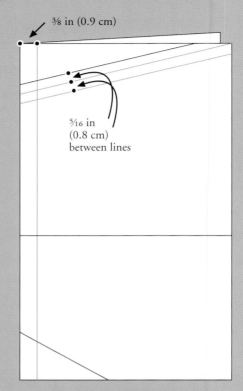

5/16 in (0.8 cm) between lines

(b)

1 Paper size: 8 ½ x 14 in (21.6 x 35.5 cm). (a) Lay paper flat in a horizontal direction. Valley fold in half vertically. Measure and draw the basic lines. (b) Measure and draw fold lines, shown in orange.

draw freehand

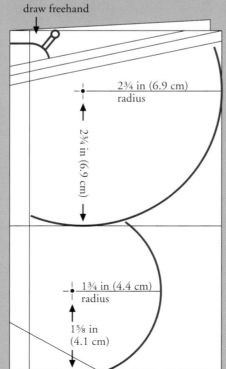

2¾ in (6.9 cm) radius

2¾ in (6.9 cm)

1¾ in (4.4 cm) radius

1⅝ in (4.1 cm)

2 Add details to head and wings, shown in green. Draw head freehand. Use the layout on p 81 for further reference.

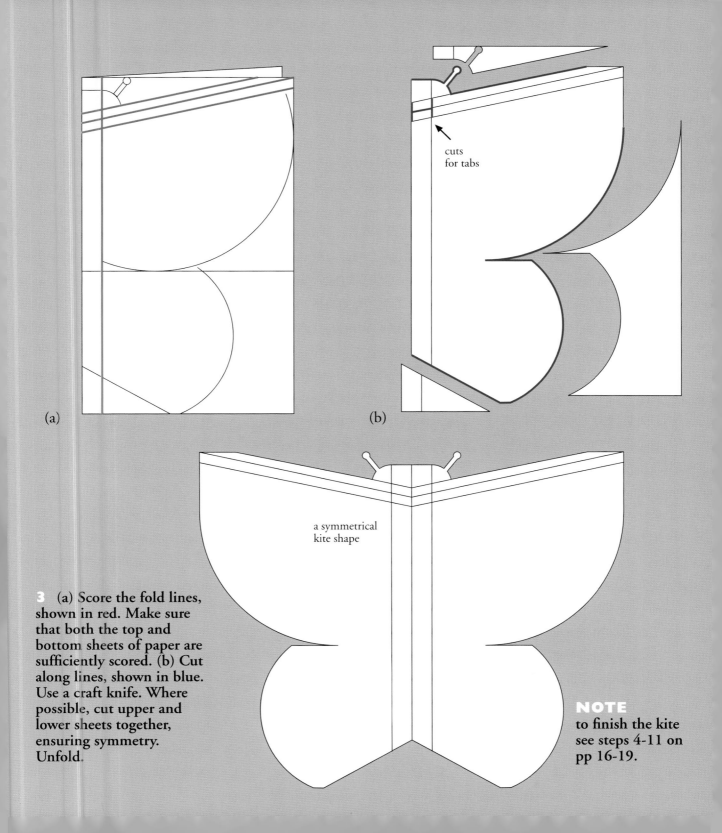

(a)

(b)

cuts
for tabs

a symmetrical
kite shape

3 (a) Score the fold lines, shown in red. Make sure that both the top and bottom sheets of paper are sufficiently scored. (b) Cut along lines, shown in blue. Use a craft knife. Where possible, cut upper and lower sheets together, ensuring symmetry. Unfold.

NOTE
to finish the kite see steps 4-11 on pp 16-19.

draw a 1 in
(2.5 cm) grid

ROSE

(with butterfly)

The rose is considered by some to be the most lovely of all flowers. Because of its beauty and fragrance, the rose represents love. It is both a wildflower and a cultivated one. When it grows wild, it is an erect or climbing shrub that bears thorns and numerous single flowers. Cultivated flowers are usually doubles. Because such lovely flowers are found on thornbushes, the rose also symbolizes the fact that there is no love in this world without pain or sorrow.

**Paper size:
8 ¹/₂ x 11 in
(21.6 x 28 cm),
folded as shown.
Decorate before
constructing the
kite.**

**Using the grid
method, copy all
or part of this
pattern to add
color to the
kite. Or create
your own
scheme.**

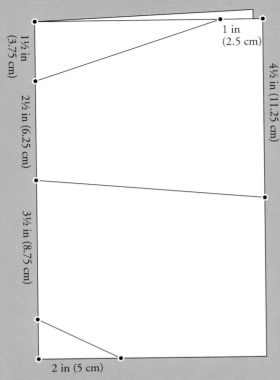

(a)

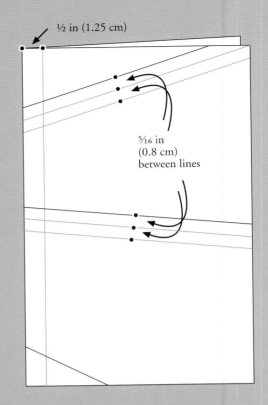

(b)

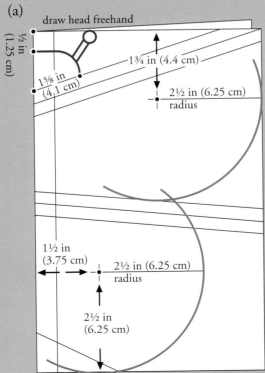

1 Paper size: 8 ½ x 11 in (21.6 x 28 cm).
(a) Lay paper flat in a horizontal direction.
Valley fold in half vertically. Measure and draw
the basic lines. (b) Measure and draw fold
lines, shown in orange.

2 Add details to head and wings, shown in
green. Draw them freehand. Use the layout on
p 85 for further reference.

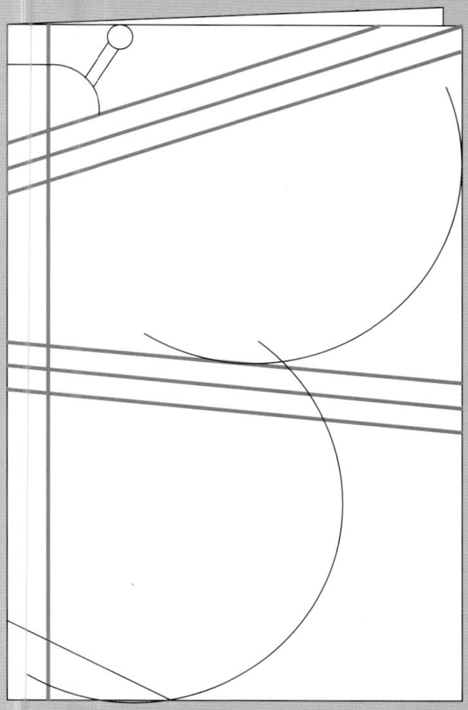

(a)

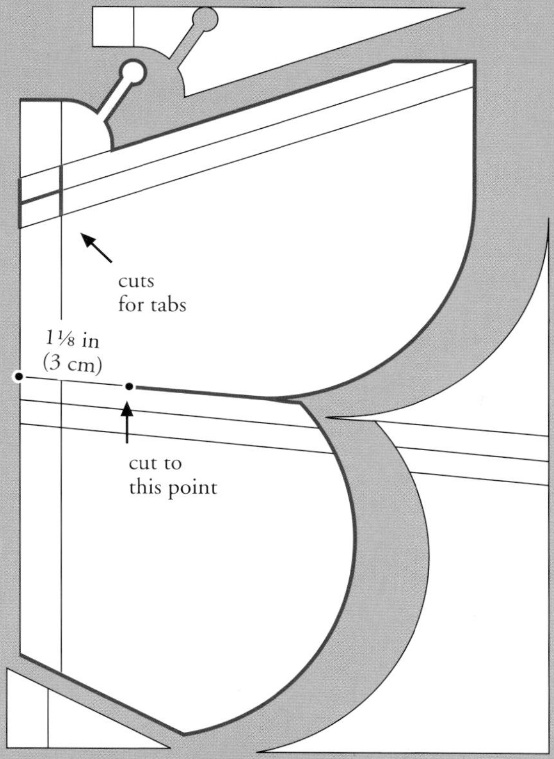

cuts
for tabs

1⅛ in
(3 cm)

cut to
this point

(b)

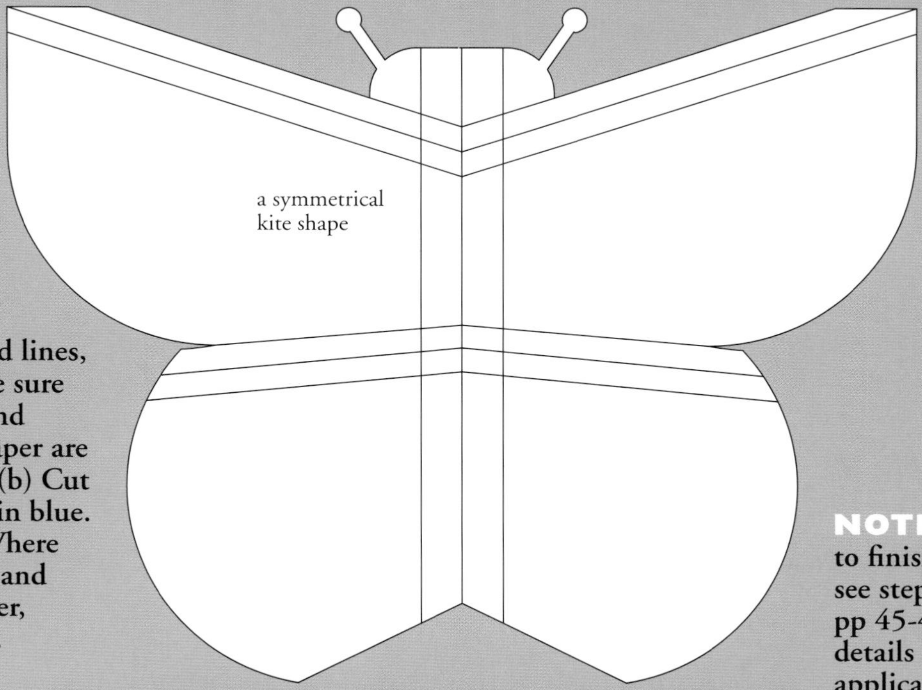

a symmetrical
kite shape

3 (a) Score the fold lines, shown in red. Make sure that both the top and bottom sheets of paper are sufficiently scored. (b) Cut along lines, shown in blue. Use a craft knife. Where possible, cut upper and lower sheets together, ensuring symmetry. Unfold.

NOTE
to finish the kite see steps 7-14 on pp 45-47, ignoring details not directly applicable.

PTEROSAUR

Pterosaurs represent the ancient past, along with their dinosaur relatives. Pterosaurs were flying reptiles that ranged in size from small ones, about the size of this kite, to giants, that were the size of small aircraft. Their leathery bat-like wings were attached to their front and back legs. Some had tails, others were tailless.

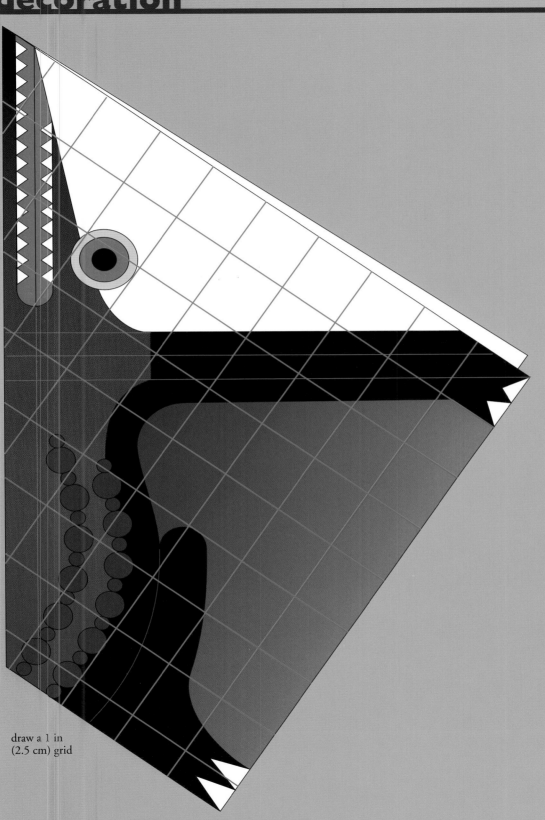

draw a 1 in
(2.5 cm) grid

**Paper size:
8 ¹/₂ x 14 in (21.6
x 35.5 cm).
Decorate before
cutting out the
kite shape.**

**Using the grid
method, copy all
or part of this
pattern to add
color to the kite.
Or create your
own scheme.**

4 in (10 cm)

4 in (10 cm)

▮ Paper size: 8 ½ x 14 in (21.6 x 35.5 cm).
Lay paper flat in a horizontal direction.
Measure and draw the basic diagonal line.
Then cut along line, shown in blue, to make
two equal pieces.

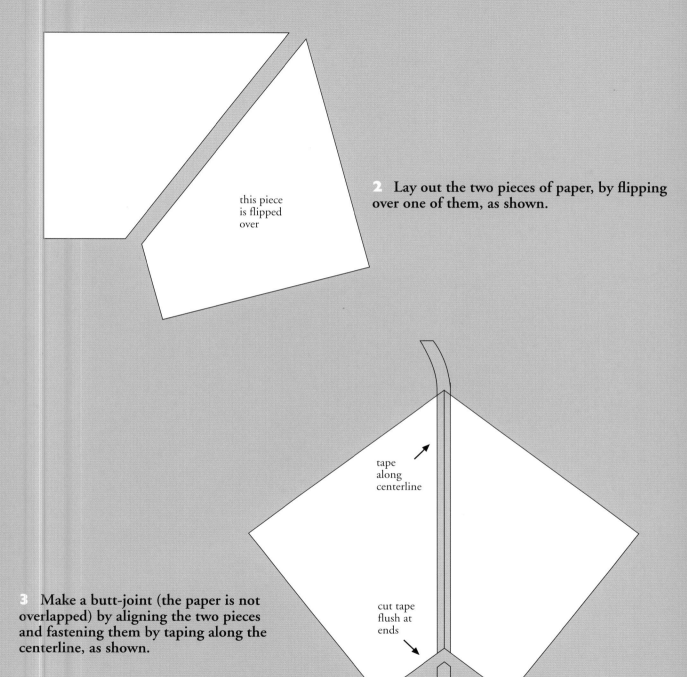

this piece
is flipped
over

2 Lay out the two pieces of paper, by flipping over one of them, as shown.

tape
along
centerline

cut tape
flush at
ends

3 Make a butt-joint (the paper is not overlapped) by aligning the two pieces and fastening them by taping along the centerline, as shown.

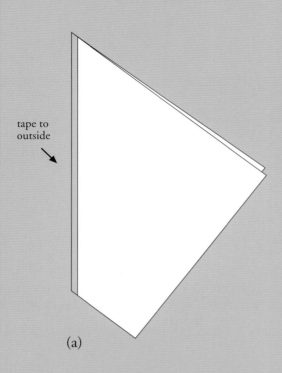

tape to
outside

(a)

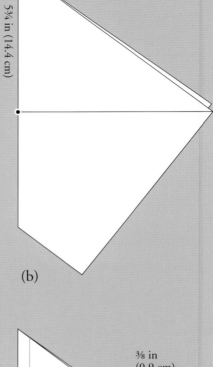

5¾ in (14.4 cm)

(b)

4 (a) Fold along centerline with the tape to the outside, as shown. (b) Measure and draw horizontal line.

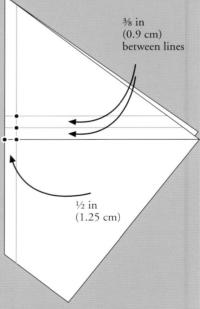

⅜ in
(0.9 cm)
between lines

½ in
(1.25 cm)

5 Measure and draw the fold lines, shown in orange.

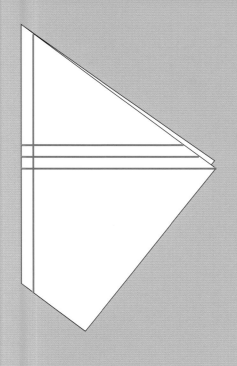

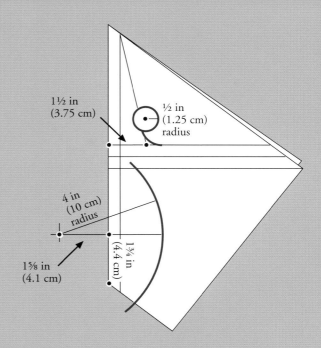

1½ in
(3.75 cm)

½ in
(1.25 cm)
radius

4 in
(10 cm)
radius

1¾ in
(4.4 cm)

1⅝ in
(4.1 cm)

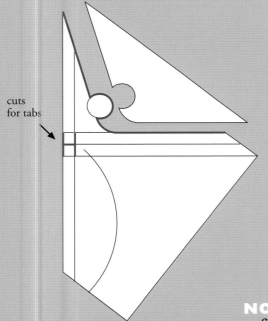

cuts
for tabs

6 Score the fold lines, shown in red. Make sure that both the top and bottom sheets of paper are sufficiently scored.

7 Measure and add details, shown in green. Use the layout on p 89 for further reference.

8 Cut along lines, shown in blue. Use a craft knife. Where possible, cut upper and lower sheets together, ensuring symmetry. Unfold.

NOTE
to finish the kite see steps 4-10 on pp 16-19, ignoring details not directly applicable.

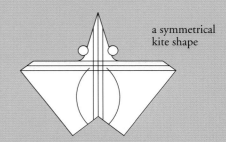

a symmetrical kite shape

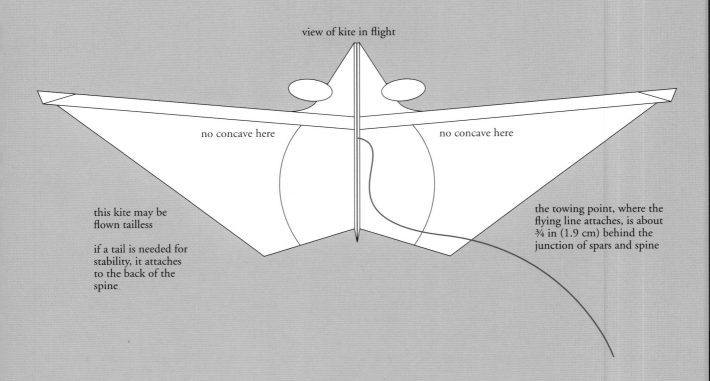

view of kite in flight

no concave here   no concave here

this kite may be
flown tailless

if a tail is needed for
stability, it attaches
to the back of the
spine.

the towing point, where the
flying line attaches, is about
¾ in (1.9 cm) behind the
junction of spars and spine

Note For best results, the kite
should be adjusted as indicated.
Make sure all glue is completely
dry before flying kite.

GLOSSARY

Angle of attack The angle of a kite as it faces the wind, higher at the leading-edge, lower at the tail end.

Airfoil A lift-producing plane (as in an airplane wing) having a curved upper surface and a less curved lower surface, which creates a pressure differential above and beneath it.

Aspect ratio The relationship between a kite's width (span from wingtip to wingtip) and its length (chord length from front to back). A square kite has a ratio of one.

Dihedral angle The upward slanting of the sail away from the spine to the wingtips.

Flying line A long length of line, stored on a reel, having one end attached to a kite's towing ring, allowing the kite to rise into the air. A kite's tether.

Keel The vertical surface found in some kites, providing yaw stability.

Pitch Rotation around a kite's lateral axis.

Roll Rotation along the length of a kite.

Sail A kite's wind-receiving surface.

Spar A framing structure that runs roughly crosswise from the spine outward.

Spine A central framing structure that runs front to back, dividing the kite into two equal halves.

Tab A small piece of material used to fasten framing pieces to the sail.

Tail A drag-creating streamer or other appendage fastened to the lower end of a kite's spine so that its drag is directly behind the kite, lending stability.

Towing point The place on the kite where the flying line is attached to give the kite the correct angle of attack.

Towing hook The hook by which the flying line is fastened to the kite.

Wind gradient The gradual increase of the speed of the wind with increasing height from the ground up.

Wind shadow The area downwind of an object where air, having passed over the object, is turbulent.

Yaw Rotation around a kite's vertical axis.

further reading

Hosking, Wayne. *Kites*. Friedman/Fairfax, New York, 1994.

Ito, Dr. Toshio, and Hirotsugu Komura. *Kites: The Science and the Wonder*. Japan Publications, Inc., Tokyo, 1983.

Jue, David. *Chinese Kites*. Tuttle, Rutland, 1967.

Pelham, David. *Kites*. Penguin, Harmondsworth, 1976.

Schmidt, Norman. *Discover Aerodynamics With Paper Airplanes*. Peguis, Winnipeg, 1991.

Schmidt, Norman. *The Great Kite Book*. Sterling/Tamos, New York, 1997.

Streeter, Tal. *The Art of Japanese Kites*. Weather Hill, New York, 1974.

Yolen, Will. *The Complete Book of Kites and Kite Flying*. Simon and Schuster, New York, 1976.

INDEX

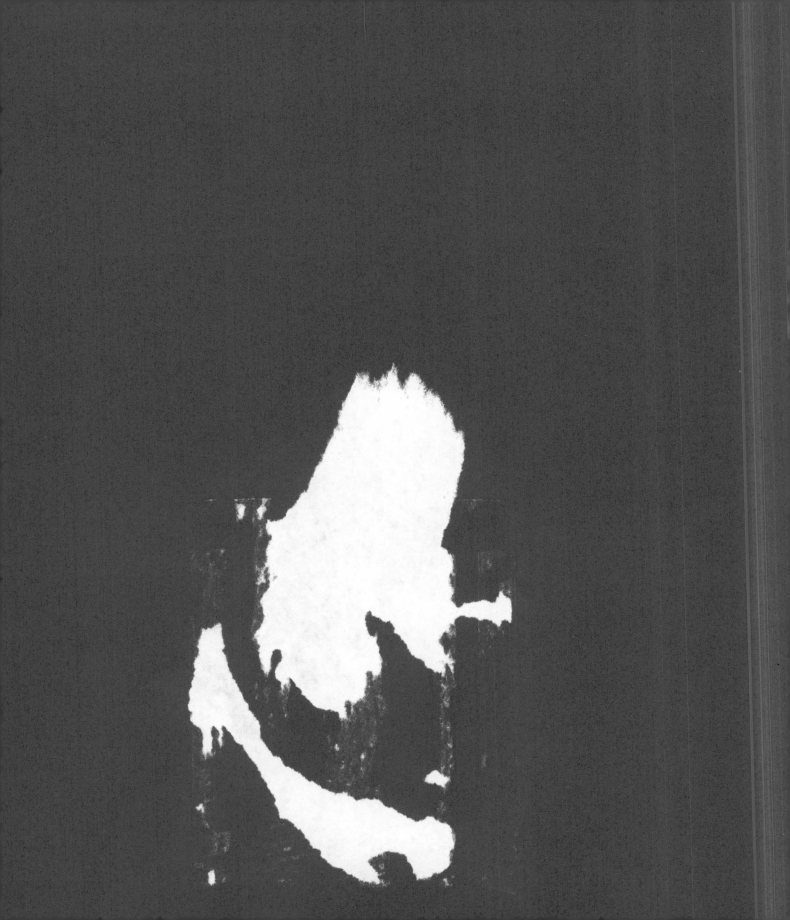